Byzantine Matters

Byzantine Matters

Averil Cameron

PRINCETON UNIVERSITY PRESS
PRINCETON AND OXFORD

Published by Princeton University Press, 41 William Street,
Princeton, New Jersey 08540

In the United Kingdom: Princeton University Press,
6 Oxford Street, Woodstock, Oxfordshire OX20 1TW

press.princeton.edu

Library of Congress Cataloging-in-Publication Data

Cameron, Averil.
Byzantine matters / Averil Cameron.
pages cm
Includes bibliographical references and index.
ISBN 978-0-691-15763-4 (hardback)
1. Byzantine
Empire—Civilization. 2. Byzantine Empire—
Historiography. I. Title.
DF521.C355 2014
949.5'02—dc23
2013034256

British Library Cataloging-in-Publication Data is available

This book has been composed in Sabon Next Pro
and Candida display

Printed on acid-free paper. ∞

Printed in the United States of America

1 3 5 7 9 10 8 6 4 2

In memory of Evelyne Patlagean

The majority has looked hitherto to that chaos of stone photography and sententious inquest on the nature of being, known as Antiquity. We, however, possessors of the twentieth century, have taken a step outside this limitation of spirit.

—Robert Byron, The Station (1931)

Byzantium, a film by Neil Jordan, 2013, described as "an atmospheric chiller about a mother-daughter vampire team."

—Ryan Gilbey, The Guardian, 28 May 2013

CONTENTS

ILLUSTRATIONS

Maps

Figures

ACKNOWLEDGMENTS

I am very grateful to Ben Tate of Princeton University Press for having prompted me to write this book. It draws on (but does not reproduce) several recent lectures and papers, and it has allowed me to follow up the ideas about Byzantium expressed in my article "The Absence of Byzantium," published in English and Greek in the monthly *Nea Hestia* (January 2008). The paper on which that article is based was given in 2007 in Peter Brown's seminar at Princeton, where I had also held a fellowship in the Program for Hellenic Studies in 2005. It was the subject of lively discussion on that occasion, and the same was also true when I gave a version in the same year in the ancient history seminar at the Institute of Classical Studies, London. Eight further issues of *Nea Hestia* between 2008 and 2009 carried comments on my paper; their authors were N. E. Karapidakis, Evangelos Chrysos, Slobodan Ćurčić, Dimitris I. Kyrtatas, Tonia Kiousopoulos, Stelianos Alexiou, Polymnia Athanassiadi, and the late and much regretted Evelyne Patlagean. I am grateful to all these scholars, and hope that they will forgive me if I have not referred to them individually or discussed all their responses in what follows. I must record my thanks here to Stavros Zoumboulakis, editor of *Nea Hestia*, for accepting my original paper and soliciting these responses, as well as to Manolis Papoutsakis for suggesting that I publish it there, and to Yannis

Papadogiannakis for his invaluable assistance with the Greek texts. I also thank Dimitri Gondicas, Stanley J. Seeger Director, Center for Hellenic Studies, Princeton, for the invitation to spend a semester at Princeton as a fellow of the Center in 2005.

I owe further thanks for help during the writing of this book to János Bak, of the Central European University, Budapest, who alerted me to the paper by Sergey Ivanov mentioned in chapter 2; to Paul Stephenson, of Radboud University, Nijmegen, whose interest in Byzantium ranges over several areas close to my own; to Katerina Ierodiakonou and Michele Trizio for their guidance in the field of Byzantine philosophy; to Gilbert Dagron, one of the greatest living Byzantinists, for his repeated kindnesses and constant inspiration; to John Haldon, also now at Princeton, for many years of Byzantine friendship; to the readers for Princeton University Press and to the editorial and production team, especially Hannah Paul, Jennifer Harris, and Sara Lerner; to James Pettifer for much travel in Byzantine lands, and for listening to me talking about things Byzantine; and to Foteini Spingou for her invaluable help in so many matters Byzantine during the past year in Oxford. My friend and colleague Judith Herrin moved from Princeton to succeed me in the chair of Late Antiquity and Byzantine Studies at King's College London that I occupied before moving to Oxford in 1994, and her book, *Byzantium: The Surprising Life of a Medieval Empire*, was also published in the United States by Princeton University Press in 2007. Two volumes of her papers on Byzantium have since followed (under the titles *Unrivalled Influence: Women and Empire in Byzantium* and *Margins and Metropolis: Authority across the Byzantine Empire*), both published in 2013, again by Princeton. Though *Byzantine Matters* adopts a very different approach, it is a good thought that we have Princeton in common too.

Finally, I must thank all those responsible for invitations to give lectures and seminars, in recent years at the British Academy; the Oxford Centre for Byzantine Research; Wolfson College, Oxford; the Royal Historical Society; the University of North Carolina, Chapel Hill; King's College London (annual symposium of the Society for the Promotion of Byzantine Studies); and the British School at Athens. The chapters in *Byzantine Matters* stand alone and were written for the present volume, but the thinking that went into these earlier papers formed an important element in their gestation.

This book offers a personal view on aspects of Byzantium and Byzantine studies that have particularly exercised me in recent years. I came to Byzantium late, after a trajectory that led me from classics to ancient history and only then to the history of Byzantium. There are those among paid-up Byzantinists who would count this a handicap. One who did not is Anthony Bryer, the only begetter and inspiration of forty-six annual British Byzantine symposia to date, and of much more besides. Working with him to establish the Society for the Promotion of Byzantine Studies in 1983 was a high point (he became its secretary, I the chair, and our president was Steven Runciman). Teaching Byzantine history at King's

College London was another experience that taught me a great deal. And I greatly value the opportunity I have had in recent years to enjoy the lively seminars, lectures, and workshops on late antiquity and Byzantium at Oxford, where "late antiquity" and "Byzantium" are generously interpreted, and no one worries, except at examination time or when budgetary matters rise to the surface, about departmental or faculty affiliations. Given the disciplinary and conceptual boundaries that are frequently mentioned in the chapters that follow, and that still stand in the way of a better understanding of Byzantium, this is precious indeed.

Averil Cameron
Oxford, September 2013

ABBREVIATIONS

Ant tard.	Antiquité tardive
BMGS	Byzantine and Modern Greek Studies
DOP	Dumbarton Oaks Papers
EHR	English Historical Review
JHS	Journal of Hellenic Studies
JÖB	Jahrbuch der Österreichischen Byzantinistik
JRA	Journal of Roman Archaeology
JRS	Journal of Roman Studies
PBSR	Papers of the British School at Rome
PG	Patrologia Graeca
REB	Revue des Études Byzantines
TIB	Tabula Imperii Byzantini
TM	Travaux et Mémoires

MAPS

Map 1. Justinian's empire, ca. 565.

Map 2. The Byzantine empire, ca. 1025.

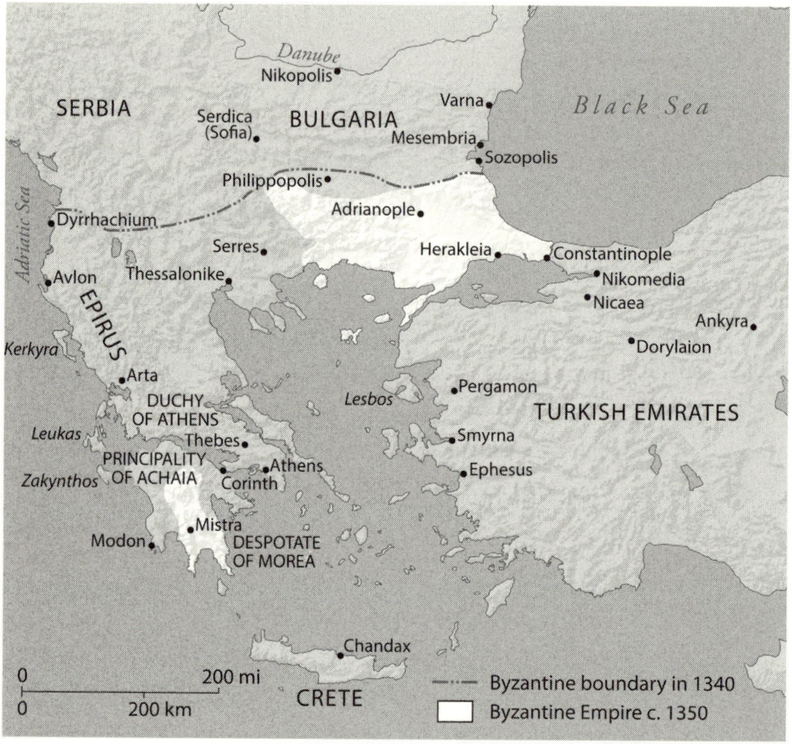

Map 3. Byzantium, ca. 1350.

Byzantine Matters

Introduction

We think we know what Byzantium was—an eastern empire ruled for hundreds of years from the city of Constantinople (Istanbul), the victim, or the duplicitous ally, of the Crusaders, the transmitter of classical culture and classical manuscripts to the west, a people tragic in their final hours before the conquest of Constantinople by the Turks in 1453, but already in a state of inexorable decline. Byzantium lies outside the standard western narrative of the formation of Europe. It is consigned to the twin spheres of exoticism and the east, and above all to the realms of ossification and pointless bureaucracy. One looks in vain for civil society in Byzantium, let alone democracy or the hallmarks of western liberalism. In the words of a distinguished Russian medievalist, "Can one imagine a Magna Carta in Byzantium or in Rus? Is it conceivable that a Byzantine emperor or a Russian tsar could view himself, or might be viewed by others, as *primus inter pares*?" The same writer continued, "However, none of this in any way lessens my admiration for scholars who are courageous enough to enter into the mysteries of Byzantine history: perhaps such people manage to overcome their own personal inclinations and sympathies."[1]

A clutch of recent publications by British and American scholars have sought to present a different, less prejudiced, and more positive view, and a series of important exhibitions has demonstrated the powerful appeal that Byzantium exerts on the wider public.[2] Yet historians of Byzantium still struggle with the weight of a powerfully negative tradition that has also made its way into common English usage. A random cull over the past few months produced allusions to "the byzantine appointments procedure" and "the Byzantine world of sports governance" (in relation to the London Olympics of 2012). Capitalization seems to be optional.

Any interpretation can only be the interpretation of its own day, and this book is inevitably written from the perspective of its author—that is, from within the Anglo-Saxon, and indeed the British, context. Interpretations of Byzantium have been and still are heavily influenced by later cultural and national agendas. The idea (and indeed the ideal) of Byzantium has a powerful salience in the Orthodox world, and has acquired even more potency with the ending of the communist regimes in eastern Europe. In Vladimir Putin's Russia a television documentary (or pseudo-documentary) with the title "The Destruction of an Empire: The Lesson of Byzantium" caused a sensation when it was shown in 2008. It had received considerable official support and went on to win a best documentary award. Its message, put crudely, was anti-western and nationalistic: Russia's true identity is as the heir of Byzantium, and it must avoid the fate of Byzantium—namely, destruction by the west.[3]

Religion is a central issue in relation to Byzantium. Few historians of the west feel confident when faced with the subject of Byzantine Orthodoxy and many prefer to relegate it to a separate sphere; at the same time in the Orthodox world the national Orthodox churches are experiencing both opportunities and problems. There are obvious tensions between the latter feature and the renewed emphasis on an exclusively western narrative of European history that has also been a recent development. The increased salience of the idea of a Christian Europe, or indeed a western world, confronted by radical Islam only adds to the discomfort surrounding Byzantium and the Orthodox sphere.

It does not help in resolving the uncertainty over Byzantium's place in historical writing today that so much of the contemporary written source material is the work of a privileged elite, or that so much Byzantine art is religious in character. Byzantium is not merely medieval but also deeply unfamiliar. Valiant efforts are needed to recapture the world of Byzantine society as a whole, and to reveal and emphasize the secular element that also existed in Byzantium (chapter 4). Reading the contemporary sources against the grain is an essential requirement.

Traditional Byzantine scholarship has flourished in a number of European centers, especially perhaps Paris, Vienna, and Munich, though also elsewhere, as well as in Greece, prerevolutionary Russia, Belgrade, and Sofia. An active group is now based in Sweden. But Byzantine scholarship was slow to gain a foothold in the Anglo-Saxon context, where it is not seen as part of our own history and needs hard-to-acquire language skills and technical expertise. It has depended in the past, moreover, on the existence of a well-established tradition of classical teaching in schools and universities, and most importantly on the teaching of classical Greek;[4] to say that this can no longer be relied upon is an understatement.[5] Furthermore, even today there are classicists who look down on Byzantium. A flood of English-language guides, general books, and translations is helping to change the situation, as are the well-attended annual conferences established since the 1960s: these include the Byzantine Studies Conference in North America and the annual British Byzantine Symposium in addition to the regular international congresses. One of the contributors to a recent handbook is confident enough to refer to "the triumph of Byzantium: Byzantine studies from the 1950s."[6] Yet the place of the subject in Anglo-Saxon universities is far from secure; it does not easily fit existing departmental structures, or feature among their priorities, and the few centers in Britain in which Byzantine studies has had an independent existence have all experienced difficulties in recent years.

To date Byzantium has only partly benefited from the enormous expansion that has taken place in the last generation in archaeological work on late antiquity, in comparison with which the archaeology of the Byzantine period proper remains at a relatively early stage. This too is changing rapidly, partly as a result of changing conceptions of the subject among Byzantinists, but also with the growth of diachronic approaches to archaeological sites and geographical areas in Greece and Turkey, which aim to trace their settlement history from the earliest times to the modern period, the Byzantine period included.

But it is also a matter of defining the period covered by "Byzantium," and here again, Byzantium as a subject finds itself in a quandary. Should it be seen as beginning with the foundation of Constantinople by Constantine I in 330, or only with the sixth or seventh century, as some Byzantinists currently prefer? French scholarship has been much less likely to see this as a problem, whether in relation to specialized publications or general introductions. This is also true of the economic history of Byzantium, in which French scholars have been prominent.[7] In Greece, too, Byzantium starts early, and late antiquity is not well established as a period of study; I will return to the reasons for this in chapter 2. Finally, in academic literature on the history and archaeology of Israel, Jordan, and to a lesser extent Egypt, "Byzantine" has traditionally meant something entirely different: the period from (roughly) the reign of Constantine until the Arab conquests of the seventh century. In contrast, an "explosion of late antiquity," as it has been called,[8] has taken hold in recent decades in the world of Anglo-Saxon scholarship. Late antiquity is now held by some scholars to embrace the rise of Islam and extend as late as the end of the first millennium, and this expansion threatens to sideline Byzantium once again. Most scholars of late antiquity would not consider themselves as Byzantinists; in contrast, many Byzantinists assume that they have a claim on the early period, even if others prefer their subject to start around the seventh century.

My aim in the chapters that follow is to highlight some of the interesting questions that arise if one tries to understand Byzantium and its society. They do not provide a history, nor do they cover all the facets that need to be addressed. Rather, they concern questions and reflections that have preoccupied me and continue to do so. I am interested throughout in methodological issues, for Byzantium is an undertheorized field as well as an understudied one.

The book consists of five essays on particular themes. I have included references to some of the secondary literature, though obviously these are highly selective, and no doubt also personal. Some of the issues I consider in this book will be familiar to my fellow-Byzantinists, though perhaps less so to others. This is not another general history of Byzantium, of which there are many already, in addition to the excellent guides and handbooks already mentioned.[9] In particular, it omits many aspects of Byzantine history and culture that would be essential to such a work. Nor is my aim to provide another apologia for Byzantium. Instead, this series of essays is designed to confront some of the issues that arise from the situation I have just outlined, and to address the question of where (if at all) Byzantium stands in relation to current historiographical trends and major historical themes, to which it often stands in a relation of tension. My hope is to explain why that should be so, and how the question can or should be tackled.

CHAPTER I

Absence

To begin with an absence may seem odd.

On the long (and more traditional) view, Byzantium lasted for over eleven hundred years, from Constantine's decision in AD 324 to found a city named after himself on the site of the ancient Greek colony of Byzantion, or from Constantinople's inauguration ceremonies in May, AD 330, to its siege and capture by the Ottomans, also in May, in 1453. That is remarkable in itself. Inevitably, however, there were major changes over such a long period, including a drastic break of nearly half a century after the sack of Constantinople by the Fourth Crusade in 1204 until Byzantine rule was restored in Constantinople under Michael VIII Palaeologus in 1261. During that time the "empire" had transferred itself to Nicaea, on the opposite side of the Bosphorus, but several other Byzantine princedoms also developed elsewhere, in Epirus, in Greece, and at Trebizond on the northern coast of Turkey. The city of Thessalonike was also a serious rival to Constantinople in the later period, especially in cultural and intellectual terms. The restored Palaeologan "empire" after 1261 was not only territorially and economically weak but also fragmented; its history is full of attempts to stave off Ottoman threats by obtaining help from the west, even at the cost of a religious union with the Roman church that few Byzantines actually wanted.

There had also been a difficult period in the seventh and eighth centuries, after the Arab conquests had deprived Byzantium of much of its eastern territory and its command of the Mediterranean. At the same time new threats had come from the north from a variety of peoples who included Slavs, Avars, Petschenigs, Khazars, and Bulgars. But Byzantium succeeded both in negotiating these dangers and in surviving an internal crisis that was at once religious and political; it also managed to reinvent itself politically, culturally, and militarily. By the tenth century the emperor Constantine VII Porphyrogenitus had the confidence to set out detailed guidance for his son on diplomatic relations with all Byzantium's neighboring peoples, and to claim to head a family of nations.[1] By the eleventh century the Bulgarians had been defeated and Bulgaria established as a Byzantine province. Contrary to earlier views, the Byzantine economy was flourishing. A new dynasty, the Comneni, again reinvented the higher offices of state, as well as the financial and military systems. The emperor Alexius I Comnenus had little choice but to cooperate with the First Crusade, and indeed entertained his own hopes of possible benefits. However, while the reasons for the sack of Constantinople by the Fourth Crusade in 1204 remain debated, the period of Comnenian rule was characterized by worsening relations with the west. Even before Alexius I took the throne in 1081, a single year, 1071, had seen both the Norman capture of the important Byzantine base of Bari in southern Italy and the Seljuk defeat and capture of a Byzantine emperor on the field at Manzikert in Asia Minor.

One thing on which all can agree is that in the end Byzantium fell to the Ottomans. How that happened is in itself a tragic story, made more so by the fact that the fate of Constantine XI, the last emperor, remains a mystery to this day.[2] The assault began in the early hours; the substantial Venetian fleet that the Byzantines hoped for failed to materialize, and after fighting bravely the Genoese commander Giustiniani was badly wounded and had to be carried off the battlefield. Mehmet II entered the city in the afternoon. The victory of the youthful sultan and his entry into the city, and especially into the church of Hagia Sophia, are enough to catch one's imagination—as is the last stand made by the small number of Byzantine inhabitants, who realized that their situation was hopeless, and the Orthodox liturgy attended by emperor and people together in Hagia Sophia on the night before the final attack.[3] But the effect of the awareness among modern historians of the coming end of Byzantium has been to lock late Byzantium into an essentialist and inexorable rhetoric of decline and victimhood. In contrast with the Roman empire, where there is room for disagreement as to when, and even if, the empire "fell," there can be no such hesitation in relation to Byzantium—the fateful date was 29 May 1453. As can be seen again and again in modern histories of Byzantium, the deeper explanation has seemed obvious: doomed to fall, Byzantium was in a state of irrevocable decline.[4] In postcolonial terms, Byzantium is the subaltern.

Yet "absence" remains an appropriate term. Part of the reason for Byzantium's absence from the wider historical discourse is that it has been relegated to the sphere of negativity. The very name that we use today—"Byzantium"—was a derogatory coinage of the early modern period, and Byzantium has traditionally been the subject of adverse comparisons with Rome and with everything classical. For Edward Gibbon, the reign of Justinian was followed by eight centuries of decline, which he compressed into a rapid survey on the grounds that the "patient reader" would find a detailed narrative intolerable. He chose instead to enliven his narrative by writing in some detail about the new peoples who came to the fore in these centuries, including his famous chapter on Muhammad and Arabia.[5] Gibbon's influence has been profound indeed, but negativity has also been shown toward Byzantium by more recent Byzantine scholars, including several recent holders of established chairs in the subject in British universities.[6] High on the list of accusations against Byzantine culture have traditionally come its alleged lack of originality and the stress laid on imitation of the classical authors, on which more later. Scholarship in the present generation is well aware of this inheritance and is doing its best to set it aside;[7] nevertheless its effects are still with us in countless standard works, and certainly in general perceptions of Byzantium. Autocracy, bureaucracy, deviousness, and a stultifying lack of originality—all still seem to go together with the word "Byzantium," underpinned by the ever-present awareness that in the end Byzantium "fell."

Some Byzantinists will argue that such ideas are happily behind us. I wish I could agree.

In general historiography, Byzantium is either nonexistent or in-between. In many Anglo-Saxon history departments Byzantium is regarded as a niche specialization, while among books intended for the general reader many of the most successful continue to emphasize court intrigue or a romanticized view of Orthodoxy. Byzantine art, and especially Byzantine icons, still exercise the same kind of fascination as they did for the American and British travelers and aesthetes in the late nineteenth and early twentieth centuries, when an important role in the discovery of Byzantium was played by men like the American Thomas Whittemore and the British Robert Byron and David Talbot Rice (figure 1).

Talbot Rice went on to become a leading Byzantine art historian, but when he and two Oxford friends and contemporaries traveled to Mount Athos in the 1920s they did so with all the enthusiasm and curiosity of Oxford undergraduates. Robert Byron's account of this journey in *The Station* was published in 1928 when the author was only 22.[8] The places he visited on his travels in 1925 and 1926 included Mistra, Athens, Constantinople, and Smyrna, and can be vividly followed in his published correspondence with his mother.[9] Byron was an Etonian who flourished in the social world of Oxford. Evelyn Waugh, another friend, but who later turned against him, described him as "short, fleshy and ugly," which chimes in with the reaction of the novelist Anthony Powell, who had known Byron at Eton: Byron was "thoroughly out of the ordi-

Figure 1. Photograph of David Talbot Rice and Mark Ogilvie-Grant at the monastery of Docheiariou on their expedition to Mouth Athos, taken by Robert Byron. ▪ Image from Robert Byron; *The Station, Athos: Treasures and Men*, reprinted by permission of Peters Fraser and Dunlop (www.petersfraserdunlop.com) on behalf of the estate of Robert Byron

nary" to look at, with "his complexion of yellowish wax, popping pale blue eyes, a long sharp nose."[10] Byron's interest in Byzantium had been roused when he saw the Ravenna mosaics while traveling in Italy at the age of eighteen. He went on to become a journalist, but while still in his early twenties he also published both *The Byzantine Achievement* (1929), which he had begun before he was twenty-one, and *The Birth of Western Painting*, with David Talbot Rice (1930), which claimed that late Byzantine art had led directly to the art of western Europe. Byron was reacting against the contemporary English Philhellenism that identified itself only with the classical in his response to what seemed the undiscovered world of Byzantium, and he was overwhelmed and excited by its mystery. We may feel that Byzantium's attraction for many of the visitors to the major Byzantine exhibitions today is not very different from what it was for Robert Byron and his Eton and Oxford friends in the early 1920s.[11]

Indeed, the very fact that Byzantium does not fit easily into western historical schemas is also a source of its attraction, as we can see not only in Yeats's often-quoted poem "Sailing to Byzantium" (1928), but also in the frequent appearances of Byzantine images in glossy advertisements today, where they are invariably associated with a glamorous world of jewelery, perfume (invariably heavy and oriental), and eastern intrigue. Byzantium has also had a powerful attraction for writers, dramatists, and composers. The empress Theodora is still a source of fascination and inspiration for novelists and even "biographers." One of the latest in a long list, is Stella Duffy's *Theodora: Actress, Empress, Whore* (2011), which was described by reviewers as "exquisite," "pulsingly vivid," and "brilliant." The cover illustration of its sequel, *The Purple Shroud* (2012) is reminiscent of the Parisian world of the late nineteenth century and the sensationally successful play *Theodora* by Victorien Sardou (1884), which had Sarah Bernhardt in the title role.[12] Since hardly anything is known about Theodora except for the famous lines in Procopius's *Secret History* that Edward Gibbon enjoyed so much, it is quite a feat to write about her yet again.[13]

So Byzantium may be present, but from the historian's point of view, it is not in the right place. It is conspicuously absent in the recent historiography of Europe, especially now, as Greece is seen as a "problem" by the powers in Brussels, and world interest is fading in the newly independent countries of southeast Europe and the Balkans. (Russia, of course, is not seen as European anyway.) Two significant contemporary phenomena have been evident: first, a shrinkage in some quarters of the concept of Europe to refer essentially to western Europe, also characterized as "Christian," and sometimes explicitly "Catholic," Europe, and second, a corresponding tendency among some historians to promote the concept of "Eurasian" over European history. "Western Eurasia" can be held to encompass Rome, and can and should encompass Byzantium; how far it does in practice, and the reasons behind the rise of the term, will be considered in the next chapter. As for understanding "Europe" as referring to western Europe, this is not new. It is further underpinned by the structure of the academic discipline of medieval history in Anglo-Saxon universities, in which, as mentioned already, Byzantium usually occupies a marginal position, if any.

We can see the effects of this very clearly from some specific historiographical examples, prominent among them the history of the Crusades. Byzantine historians have long felt that the Byzantine perspective needed to be reflected in the huge secondary literature, and it found a sympathetic voice in the early 1950s in Steven Runciman's three-volume *History of the Crusades*.[14] In her history of the reign of her father, Alexius I Comnenus, the Byzantine historian Anna Comnena vividly conveys the impression made in Constantinople at the first encounter of the Byzantines by the seemingly uncouth westerners (who had so recently captured the Byzantine city of Bari in south Italy). However, Anna was writing with hindsight, and her father, Alexius I, did his best to manage this new challenge.[15] Nevertheless, mutual hostility between Byzantines and Latins grew over the next century, and even led to the expulsion of Latins from Constantinople in the 1180s.

The defining moment came in 1204, when, for whatever reason, the Fourth Crusaders turned on Constantinople and sacked it. Latin rule was established with a Latin "emperor" and a Latin patriarch and the Byzantine court and administration driven into exile. Almost worse was the desecration of holy places and pillaging of what Byzantine believed to be the holiest objects in Christendom—the relics of the Passion of Christ. As a result the crown of thorns is now in Notre Dame in Paris, while other relics, including the miraculous image of Christ known as the Mandylion, taken to Constantinople in 944 from Edessa (now Sanliurfa in the far east of Turkey), were housed in the specially built Sainte Chapelle, where they eventually fell victim to the French Revolution. Yet a western medievalist writing on the Crusades regards the lurid, but, we might think, justified, eyewitness accounts of the brutal sack of the city by Nicetas Choniates and Nicholas Mesarites as "hysterical."[16] There is plentiful evidence of actual coexistence between Latins and Orthodox in the Crusader kingdoms, but on the religious and political level the Byzantines felt threatened, even after the Byzantine court and government were reestablished in Constantinople in 1261. It is a commonplace in the voluminous Greek literature produced during the debates about the union of the churches that the Latin participants in the debates were arrogant and quick to score points.

A second example also involves east versus west, this time the split between eastern and western Christianity. Attempts had already been made to resolve the differences between the Roman Catholic and Orthodox churches, especially after the heated interchanges in 1054 (no longer regarded by historians as a real "schism" but certainly presaging future problems). After the Byzantine return to Constantinople in 1261 these differences rose to a new level of urgency within both the ecclesiastical and secular elites in Byzantium, though always accompanied by deep disagreement. For urgent political reasons, the emperor Michael VIII Palaeologus drove through a divisive agreement at the Council of Lyons in 1274 that was never likely to last. Many papal delegations came and debated in high-profile encounters with Byzantines. Countless treatises were composed on both sides. By the final days of Byzantium the need for western support was overwhelming, but it came at a high price, with recognition of papal supremacy at the top of the list. The Council of Ferrara/Florence in 1438–39 involved large delegations on both sides, and was held in complex circumstances. Its result was predictable, a declared union of the churches that provoked yet more opposition in Constantinople. Several prominent Byzantines converted to Catholicism and were rewarded by being made cardinals. The princely courts and towns of Italy were also no doubt more attractive than the dangerous situation at home. But the Byzantine side could have done better had they done more homework on the works by Latin theologians marshaled in evidence by the western speakers. In any case the vaunted union, despite its vast effort and expense, did not hold, and proved as deceptive as the hoped-for support against the Ottomans. Constantinople fell soon afterward, and an Orthodoxy even more strongly demarcated from Roman Catholicism became the badge of Greek identity within the Ottoman empire.

Dealing with these debates and divisions, which went on for several centuries, has proved difficult for historians of Byzantium. It may be unfair to speak of a western triumphalist perspective, yet many of the scholars who have engaged with the subject and the contemporary source material have indeed—consciously or not—written from a western, or indeed a Roman Catholic, standpoint.[17] Some Byzantine historians are acutely aware of the problem,[18] and fueled by what is perceived as Orthodox failure, such Roman Catholic negativity toward Byzantium has also naturally led to an apologetic tendency among Orthodox theologians.[19] Added to this, most guides and handbooks to the eastern church are written from within the Orthodox tradition, while many key contemporary texts still lack modern critical editions, or even remain unpublished. In a more extreme step, a few Orthodox scholars have argued that westerners are unable in principle to understand Orthodox theology or the Orthodox position.[20] Nor is the bias only between Catholic and mainstream Orthodox: to quote one recent writer dealing with theological discussions between Byzantium and the Armenians in the twelfth century, "unfortunately from the point of view of objective scholarship those who have studied Nerses' agenda [Nerses IV, head of the Armenian church, 1167–73] have tended to have their own particular Christological axe to grind and wish to prove him 'orthodox' in accordance with their individual notions of what constitutes orthodoxy."[21]

The pervasive role played by Orthodoxy in Byzantium is one of the features that have made the history of Byzantium so difficult to write (figure 2). Some historians have reacted by adopting reductionist agendas or writing theology out of the story as much as possible.[22] In other cases, for authors from Arnold Toynbee to Samuel Huntington, "Orthodoxy" or "Orthodox civilization" has acquired a status of its own, not western, and not quite eastern, but also (like Islam in these scenarios) not European, and therefore not enlightened. The real or potential agendas behind such a view are

Figure 2. The watercolors of Mount Athos by Edward Lear (d. 1888) convey the romantic appeal it had for Byron. Talbot Rice's purpose on their expedition in 1927 was to photograph the frescoes in the monasteries and where possible record their treasures, which were hardly known at the time. ▪
Mount Athos, The Monastery of St. Paul, 1858, Edward Lear (1812–88) / Private Collection / Photo © The Fine Art Society, London, UK / The Bridgeman Art Library

obvious; they also complicate the place of Byzantium within current thinking about global, transnational, or comparative history. I will return to the subject in the next chapter and in chapter 5.

My third example concerns the late, Palaeologan, period, after Michael VIII Palaeologus had reestablished Byzantine rule in the capital (though indeed it was hardly his own achievement). Small and fragmented though Byzantium now was, as well as "decaying," "feeble," or even "doomed," and although individuals still prized ancient authors and rhetorical display above such modernizing ideas as originality, intellectual life in Constantinople, Thessalonike, and Mistra reached an astonishingly high level. Byzantine scholars enthusiastically collected, copied, and edited classical texts and Latin classical authors were translated into Greek: in the theological sphere Augustine's *On the Trinity* and the works of Aquinas also became available in Greek in Constantinople, while at the beginning of the fifteenth century Manuel Chrysoloras taught and translated Greek texts in several Italian cities, including Florence and Rome. Other Byzantines were also attracted by what seemed to be happening in Italy. Was this Byzantine intellectual activity a "renaissance," or even the first stirring of "the" Renaissance?[23] The end of Byzantium did indeed mean that the collections and libraries of Italy were filled with classical manuscripts, and some of the last Byzantines were themselves great collectors.[24] But the privileging of Italian humanism and the western tradition has usually assigned to Byzantium the essentially passive role of transmitter.

Byzantinists point out that the classical tradition had never been lost in Byzantium, and that while the period from 1204 to 1261 certainly represented a "setback," cultural and intellectual life was maintained or even strengthened during this period, and high-level education reestablished in Constantinople after 1261. However, while there was undoubtedly a revival of learning, calling it a renaissance confuses the issue. Earlier Byzantine "renaissances" have also been promoted: a "Macedonian renaissance" in the tenth century under the Macedonian dynasty, a twelfth-century renaissance, and an earlier revival of learning starting around AD 800. But the term "renaissance" is problematic in all these cases, while for late Byzantium the social framework of the Italian cities was a world away.[25] Like Byzantine philosophy, often simply subsumed in modern scholarship into theology (chapter 5), late Byzantine intellectuals and the integrity of their engagement with the Italian cities deserve to be given an autonomous voice. Younger Byzantinists already know this, but negative views can still be found within Byzantine scholarship. The great Byzantinist Ihor Ševčenko appreciated the learning of these intellectuals, whose number he put at 150 or 200, revised upward from his earlier estimate, but compared them adversely with Italian humanists of the fifteenth century (as merely "Christian" or "surface" humanists); others are far less generous.[26]

I will end this chapter with a set of issues already well known to Byzantinists, but which are also germane to my theme.

When the city of Constantinople was founded, it was part of the eastern Roman empire, and the two parts, east and west, had yet to diverge. Latin was still in use in Constantinople in the sixth century, but the main language, and the language of intellectual culture, in the east was already Greek, and while Latin soon fell away, Greek remained the primary language throughout the long history of Byzantium. But the kind of Greek that was the language of Byzantine culture became more and more separate from the spoken language, and its acquisition depended on an educational system based on rhetorical accomplishment, with a very high premium placed on technical skill.[27] Within the field of theological literature (of which there was a vast amount), a similar premium was placed on the works of the Fathers of the Church who wrote in Greek—authorities like Basil of Caesarea, Gregory of Nazianzus, and John Chrysostom (known to modern Orthodoxy as "the three hierarchs"). If there seemed to be disagreements between these or others of the Fathers, they had to be explained away, for the Fathers could not be admitted to differ. In addition, Byzantine ecclesiastics and theologians had often received an excellent classical training themselves. They sometimes found it hard to combine the two influences, but many succeeded in doing so.

Nothing could be further from the value placed by our own society on originality and creativity, and these features of Byzantine intellectual life have given rise to many derogatory judgments from modern scholars.[28] At the heart of the problem is the premium placed in Byzantium on *mimesis* ("imitation"), generally taken as referring to the value placed on the imitation of classical literary works.[29] As far as Byzantine literature is concerned, the issue is only partially alleviated in the light of current debates about *mimesis* among literary theorists, who see the relation of one literary text to another in far more complex and shifting terms.[30] Again, we can observe an apologetic note, as Byzantine literary scholars try to find ways of presenting their subject in a less derogatory light.[31] This has at various times involved attempting to find actual signs of originality, looking for evidence of humor in this apparently highly serious society,[32] or emphasizing its nonreligious sides. Equally modernizing are publications focusing on gender (eunuchs as well as women, and children as well as adults). The lower classes are less visible in the contemporary sources than the educated elite, but they too have been an object of attention recently, as has "daily life." The language of one reviewer of the volume from which these examples are taken makes the size of the gap between these and more traditional approaches abundantly clear, referring to "almost incomprehensible oratory," "unreadable epistolography," and the need to "entertain the possibility that in some periods the level of artistic or literary achievement was higher or lower than in others"—that is, to admit that "some Byzantine art is poorly executed" and "some Byzantine literature is poorly written."[33]

Byzantine literature at present constitutes a particular point of tension, but also a *locus* of new approaches, as ways are sought of interpreting texts that seem on the surface to be intractable.[34] An emphasis on performance and performativity—oral performance, especially in private salons (*theatra*)—over reading is currently overtaking rhetoric as key to elite literary activity. However, actual evidence for *theatra* is very unevenly spread over the period,[35] and an emphasis on performance suits certain kinds of writing more than others—orations, for example, or poetry, or indeed homilies, or literary epistolography or rhetorical display pieces. A close link always existed between literary production and patronage, and demonstrable rhetorical skill was essential in order to attract an influential patron and provide the route to a good career. The court, the administration, and the church all had interests in the educational "system" (in fact, a network of private schools built around particular teachers). These "schools" produced and supported this emphasis on competitive rhetorical skill, especially in the eleventh and twelfth centuries, at times holding interschool competitions of their own, and again in the Palaeologan period, both periods when high-level literary production was at its height.[36]

But this may not be the whole story. Not surprisingly, perhaps, many "literary" discussions of Byzantine literature focus on the works that seem easier to manage for a modern critic: satirical texts in prose and verse—for example, the small corpus of Byzantine "novels" in the manner of earlier works of the same type—and increasingly, the writing of poetry. The twelfth century attracts special attention as a well-documented period that seems to have seen a new kind of literary activity with many surviving examples. Some have even seen in this the beginnings of modern Greek literature.

But despite the "linguistic turn" and the rise of literary theory there is still no comprehensive literary history of Byzantium to replace the classic handbook of Byzantine secular literature by Herbert Hunger, published in 1978.[37] The missing element is always theological writing (and it is hard to imagine many theological treatises being "performed"), yet theologians were authors too, and the very people who wrote in a secular vein often also wrote theological treatises, dialogues, and other such works (chapter 5).

How can we make sense of this complex and in many ways unfamiliar society, which seems to need so much preliminary explanation? Does it need to be rescued, as some modern specialists evidently think, and if so, why?

CHAPTER 2

Empire

Was Byzantium an empire?

It is almost always referred to as such, as "the Byzantine empire," despite the attempt of a recent writer to rebrand it as "the city-state of the Romans."[1] After all, Byzantium had an "emperor," even though he had been referred to since the seventh century, and even earlier, as *basileus*, the Greek term for "king." The language of court and culture was Greek, but the Byzantines did indeed claim to be, and called themselves, Romans, the heirs of the undivided Roman empire. These contradictions still have a resonance in modern Greece and in the scholarship on Byzantium, and will be discussed further in the next chapter.

The reign of Justinian (AD 527–65) seems at first sight to mark a decisive stage. Whether or not this was his original intent, Justinian's "reconquest" aimed to recover the western territories that been lost from Roman rule since the fifth century, and so restore a unified Roman empire, albeit one ruled from Constantinople. His initiative was only partly successful even in the short term. Even before the Arab conquests of the seventh century the political reunification of east and west was shown to be no more than a dream.[2] Justinian and his immediate successors were also deeply engaged with religious differences in the east and with the military threat posed by the Sasanians. Perhaps Justinian's greatest achievement was the immense task of codifying the entire body of Roman law (in Latin); this became the basis of the later legal compilations that served the Byzantine empire. Not surprisingly, Edward Gibbon was unsure about whether Justinian was to be regarded as "Roman" or consigned to the long line of "Greek" emperors who followed him.

But Byzantine interests in Italy continued, even if wider political reunification failed, and despite a rearguard action by some historians to lay emphasis on the traditional idea of a final "fall" of the Roman empire in the west in the late fifth century,[3] the cultural and economic ties that linked the different parts of the Mediterranean world continued at least until the seventh century and in significant ways beyond it. This kind of change came at a slow pace, not with a big bang, and in ways that affected the east as well as the west.[4]

Byzantium has suffered from what an Italian historian writing in 1999—nearly thirty years after the publication of Peter's Brown's book, *The World of Late Antiquity*, in 1971—called the "explosion" of late antiquity as a historical period.[5] In Brown's book, late antiquity was already defined as continuing until AD 750, and a more recent tendency extends the upper limit even further, sometimes as far as AD 1000. Either way, the effect is to dissolve conventional divisions between the ancient and medieval worlds, and to draw Byzantium (and now also Islam) into a broader "late antique" world in which issues of state power and the history of institutions yield place to social and cultural factors, similarity and continuity. Seen in this way, late antiquity does not easily fit discussions about empire, and with its shifting contours and fluid social formations Brent Shaw indeed sees the period as marking the end of a "Mediterranean world-system," "a great geo-political shift," and a time of fragmentation.[6] Byzantium is not easy to accommodate within either frame.[7] Deeming Byzantium to begin only in the sixth or seventh century, as some Byzantinists prefer,[8] does not help in the light of the longer definitions of late antiquity now current. The long late antique periodization, even including early Islam in its purview, does not merely problematize the chronology of Byzantium; it also obscures the place of Byzantium in discussions of empire and empires.

The same is true of another recent historiographical tendency, which seeks to avoid the crime of "Eurocentricity"[9] by locating Byzantium within a much wider entity conceived as western Eurasia. This poses some new difficulties,[10] and again, the particularity of Byzantium is a casualty, this time to the anxiety of historians to avoid the traditional comparison between Byzantium and western Europe.[11] Behind this debate lies the much deeper issue of the assumed advances made by the west and the supposed backwardness of the east. Where does Byzantium stand in relation to this polarity? Similar, if not greater, difficulties lie in attempts to bring Byzantium into global or transnational history, and so far the most active exploration of this model has come less from Byzantinists than from historians of the Roman empire. The porousness of Byzantium's borders, insofar as they existed as such (for the efforts made by the Roman empire to establish defended borders were not continued in the Byzantine period), meant that the contours of the Byzantine state were particularly liable to shift along with the rise and fall of neighboring peoples.[12] Its imperial reach was often ill-defined and its extent varied greatly over time. But this should make it more, rather than less, suited to the transnational approach. Indeed, one of the stated aims of a new center for global history at Oxford (in the planning of which Byzantium has been well represented) is to explore the dialogue between imperial, transnational, and comparative history.

Empires, and the fall of empires, have attracted lively attention from historians since the collapse of the Soviet Union, and in relation to the "American empire." Among the topics discussed are the techniques of imperial and colonial rule, the factors making for continuity or the opposite in imperial systems and their advantages or disadvantages for their subjects. The nature of ruling elites is another frequent theme. Ancient empires are also a current subject of comparative history, with Rome and China as the main empires compared.[13] The latter comparison is traditional, and the availability of certain kinds of data, as well as certain structural similarities, makes it an obvious one, but again Byzantium is usually excluded; Haldon is right to point out that Byzantium has hardly been analyzed so far in terms of power, empire or state-formation.[14] A recent book by the military strategist Edward Luttwak aims to apply to Byzantium the same kind of political and military analysis he had used in relation to Rome in the 1970s.[15] But there are problems with his analysis,[16] and he does not extend his coverage beyond 1204, when Constantinople was sacked by the Fourth Crusade and a short-lived Latin "empire" set up. One can understand why Luttwak ended at this point, and indeed, current scholarship emphasizes the fragmentation of Byzantine rule that followed and the weakness of the restored Palaeologan state after 1261. A good case can be made for considering Byzantium in this period as a premodern princely society. But the Byzantines themselves thought otherwise. In fact this last period of Byzantium was one in which not only the role played by court patronage in intellectual life but also the imperial ideology reached new heights.[17]

The term "empire" clearly needs to be defined, and its application to Byzantium given a clear chronological range. Of course neither of these caveats matters if Byzantium itself is overlooked.

A basic definition of empire would probably include the ability to bring disparate and "foreign" elements under central control, as well as the capacity to exploit population and territory by exacting some form of tribute ("tributary states"). Centralization of the means of exploitation is crucial ("state power"),[18] and the key items of expenditure from the wealth that is extracted in this are likely to consist in the maintenance of an army and of the governing structures, including the court and the display that this entails. In writing of the early period Haldon usefully speaks of "different shades of stateness," and refers to Byzantium as "a mature state";[19] it seems clear that—if sometimes only with difficulty—it was able to retain its status as a tributary state at least until the sack of 1204.

The Roman empire certainly also qualifies on this basis, especially when at its height in the first and second centuries AD, but the case of Byzantium is in fact more complex. When the emperor Constantine founded the city he called Constantinople, it was not as the capital city of a discrete new empire, but as his personal seat, not unlike the "capitals" established by his own father and his rivals at Trier, Thessalonike, and Serdica (modern Sofia). It was the special prerogatives, largesse, and other advantages bestowed on it by Constantine and his successors that gradually established Constantinople's position. By the sixth century its population exceeded that of Rome several times over.[20] It was slow to become the city of churches and monasteries that it became in later periods. But the failure of Justinian's attempt to recover Rome for the long term and Constantinople's success in fending off dangerous sieges by the Avars and Persians and then the Arabs in the seventh and eighth centuries meant that its status as the capital was unquestioned. Much later, when the emperor and administration had been forced to leave Constantinople in 1204, and more than one Byzantine outpost was established, it was taken for granted that one day there must be a return to the city and the reestablishment of Byzantine government there. Whether with hindsight that was realistic, given the circumstances of the thirteenth century, is open to debate, but the return of Michael VIII Palaeologus to Constantinople from "exile" in Nicaea, when he staged an entrance into the city on foot behind the great icon of the Virgin Hodegetria, was undoubtedly one of the great moments in Byzantine history.

The adaptability of elites and governing structures in Byzantium was one of the empire's greatest strengths. Late antiquity was a period of change and fluidity, which saw enormous shifts in the extent of territory ruled from Constantinople. New states emerged in the west and the north, and the Arab conquests established Islamic rule around the Mediterranean. The eventual outcome of this realignment was far from clear. With the loss of so much Byzantine territory went a consequent collapse in tax revenues and in the administrative structure that had served the late Roman empire and early Byzantium so well. The details remain very obscure, yet over the period from the late seventh to ninth centuries the governing elite was successfully restructured, with new titles and organization, and a new tax system and military structure put in place, designed to deal with changed conditions and a much higher degree of local instability. The new system took shape in circumstances of contraction, but proved adaptable enough to extend to other areas as the center of gravity also changed; the achievement that these changes represent was enormous.[21] Byzantium reorientated itself of necessity toward the north and northwest, and the eighth-century emperors set about the necessary adaptation, including the repopulation of the capital. During the same period the Roman lawcodes inherited from the great work of Justinian in the sixth century were revised and adapted in two new compilations. These changes are all the more remarkable in that while they were taking shape the empire survived a dangerous siege of the capital by the Arabs, a long internal dispute over the status of religious images, and the threat of usurpation. Constantine V (d. 775) was also able to campaign against the Arabs in the east, resettle some of the Christian population previously under Arab rule, and make war on the Bulgarians in the Balkans.

By the tenth century a new administrative arrangement was in place, whereby officials were rewarded by *rogai*, effectively salaries, in a highly monetarized and centralized system that rewarded government service and supported the imperial office (even when the throne itself was contested, as it often was). It amounted to a centralized bureaucracy, tied in to the imperial court and its ceremonies by patronage.[22] Thus Byzantium was characterized by reliance on a service aristocracy rather than an aristocracy of birth. In the late eleventh century a new imperial dynasty, the Comneni, arose from among the emerging great landowning families of the period,[23] and appointed members of its own family and circle to a range of new offices and titles, perhaps creating what can fairly be called an aristocracy. However, only one eleventh-century Byzantine author uses that term, and he applies it rather to the ranks and titles held by the court elite before the establishment of the Comnenian system of the late eleventh century. The term "aristocracy" is also used, for instance, by Peter Sarris to apply to the great landowners of the sixth century who were at the center of the more monetarized economy he sees operating in that period, and with whom the emperors had an uneasy relationship.[24] In other words, when the term "aristocracy" is used by modern writers on Byzantium it tends to be used in a loose sense; the great families that emerged in the eleventh century and later were not "aristocratic" in the strict sense, and their hold on their position was by no means guaranteed.

The centuries after Justinian saw a major readjustment in Byzantine elites; it remained a striking feature of the Byzantine elites both secular and ecclesiastical that membership depended less on birth than on other factors. Families could not preserve status by heredity alone, though they did their best to do so. This can be vividly seen from the attempts of the Comnenian imperial network to evade church legislation restricting kinship marriage (and so to keep wealth and status within the family group). From the eleventh century onward, a recovery of urban life also led to the emergence of local *archontes*, a middling elite of landowners who might or might not also have ties to richer and more powerful "magnates." Neither group constituted a feudal aristocracy. At the higher urban level, possession of a superior level of literary culture was the essential key to social mobility. This was recognized and fostered by the emperors, who took pains to provide for the availability of higher learning by founding new institutions and posts. At these higher levels, Byzantine society was highly competitive, and in the Palaeologan period, after 1261, we find many illustrations of the doors, both secular and ecclesiastical, that were opened to the recipients of this higher learning; they included individuals whose careers spanned both secular teaching positions and ecclesiastical office.

Such flexibility on the part of Byzantine elites over many centuries, the central role played by imperial patronage, and the capacity of the state to reinvent itself even while retaining the imperial office and ideology are a very far cry from the unchanging Byzantium of popular myth. The extent to which these elites were radically different from the ones that had gone before, or whether essentially similar groups were reformed and renamed, is a difficult one.[25] But what matters is that such flexibility and adaptability should have continued for so long.

In some periods in its long history the very existence of Byzantium was under threat. Yet though the mechanisms changed over time, and military resources were sometimes very short, ways were found to extract a surplus, maintain a court, field an army, and even make territorial gains. It has been suggested that Byzantium's status as an empire is anomalous, partly because its history was more a history of contraction than of imperial expansion.[26] Edward Luttwak in turn identifies the doctrine of relying on diplomacy and avoiding unnecessary war as characteristic of Byzantium. Yet in the tenth century Byzantium was able to recover territory in Asia Minor and farther east that had been lost earlier to the Arabs, and in the eleventh century the successful campaigns of Basil II, "the Bulgar-slayer," were followed by the incorporation and organization of Bulgaria (essentially corresponding to what is currently known as FYROM, part of former Yugoslavia) as a Byzantine province (figure 3). Byzantium maintained provincial rule in parts of Italy, in Ravenna in the north until the eighth century and Bari in the south until 1071, and at its height the provincial and military theme system covered the Balkans and was extended and developed by the tenth century to cover much of Asia Minor. While not perhaps constituting the conquest of foreign peoples, this testifies to expanding territorial ambitions and to success in extending the reach of imperial control. The rise of the Italian trading cities provided new opportunities for Byzantium, and they were granted concessions in Constantinople itself. The factor that most constrained further expansion was the impact of new threats and new potential enemies, including in the later period the establishment of the Seljuks, and later the Ottomans, in Asia Minor. But another factor, which is often overlooked, is the degree to which Byzantium was able to manage its provincial government by moving populations when necessary, as well as its success in incorporating the populations that came within its control. Byzantium was particularly vulnerable to changes in external conditions, with new peoples and new states emerging around it. But in total, the various changes over time in the Byzantine system illustrate rather well the applicability of the neo-Darwinian approach to empires as "determined by competitive selection of social, ideological and political-institutional practices."[27]

The characteristics of empires, once they have come into existence by the conquest of territory and established a unified central

Figure 3. The cathedral of St. Sophia at Ohrid, dating back to the eleventh century. After the Byzantine reconquest of what was then known as Bulgaria in 1018, Ohrid became the seat of Byzantine archbishops, who included Theophylact of Ohrid in the late eleventh century and Demetrius Chomatenus in the thirteenth (when Ohrid belonged to the Despotate of Epirus). ▪ Image © vlas2000 / shutterstock.com

administrative system, have been expressed by one scholar as consisting of their capacity to administer and exploit diversity, the existence of a transportation system designed to serve the imperial center militarily and economically and of systems of communication allowing administration of the subject areas from the center, the assertion of a monopoly of force within their territories, and an "imperial project" that imposed some type of unity throughout the system.[28] We might add to this list the existence of a legal framework. Byzantium had all of these, even though it grew out of an earlier imperial system, and its territorial extent varied greatly over time. It also demonstrated a remarkable determination to maintain itself, through the continuity of imperial office and ideology (including religious ideology, which will be the subject of chapter 5), sustained by a learned culture, access to which the emperors themselves sought to control. It maintained this symbolic continuity even in the face of the constant instability of the throne itself.

Consideration of Byzantium as an empire has been complicated by the model of a "Byzantine commonwealth," put forward by Dimitri Obolensky in his well-known book published with that title in 1971.[29] On this view, for much of its history Byzantium exercised a kind of "soft power," based on its reputation and standing, and often, if not quite always, associated with its role as the home and champion of eastern Orthodoxy. In 1993 Garth Fowden applied the same concept, as "the first Byzantine commonwealth," to the relations of Constantinople with other states and peoples in the eastern Mediterranean from Constantine until the age of the Abbasids, also positing an Islamic commonwealth, especially after the collapse of Abbasid power, and even a Latin commonwealth in the west as a further member of "late antiquity's legacy of commonwealths."[30] According to him, this was "late antiquity's contribution to the technique of empire," and its "invention" came as a result of the monotheism adopted by Constantine. It follows that this "commonwealth" was implicated from the start in a religious ideology; when applied to the post-Byzantine period the idea is even more closely associated with the influence of Orthodoxy, and especially that of the monastic milieu of Mount Athos during the Ottoman period.

The term "commonwealth" has also attracted some criticism.[31] Its topdown implications of Byzantium's "legacy" or influence are less persuasive in a postcolonial world, where horizontal exchange and plurality are emphasized more than a topdown "handing-on." We need now to look less to the religious agendas emphasized in previous scholarship than to "connective history"—networks, connections, and interacting systems, including trade, diplomacy, and indeed these aspects of religion.[32]

Jonathan Shepard has cautiously endorsed the term "commonwealth" in several important contributions, but has proposed a somewhat different model, in terms of overlapping circles, or "force-fields." He has memorably described Byzantium as "an empire of the mind," a "politico-cultural sphere," within the three overlapping circles of influence in geographical terms: "the Byzantine commonwealth," the Christian and Islamic Orient, and Latin Christendom.[33]

But Byzantium's reach was wider than what became the Orthodox sphere, and contested and complex even there.[34] Even leaving aside Eurasian or global historical conceptions, Byzantium needs to be understood within its wider relationships. Moreover, the term "commonwealth" is inherently favorable, bypassing considerations of power and social macrostructures in favor of a kind of generalized cultural beneficence. Yet, as also argued by Shepard, Byzantium did not hesitate to deploy military force in order to conquer or reconquer territory in the very period when its rhetoric of benign headship was at its strongest.[35]

The understanding of Byzantium suffers from decades of *idées reçues.* Even now in many countries, especially in the Balkans, the standard one-volume history of Byzantium remains that of George Ostrogorsky, originally published in German in 1940 by a Russian émigré who became a student in Germany and moved to Belgrade in 1934, where he spent the rest of his career.[36] The book has a Slavist agenda, especially in relation to the so-called "dark ages" of the seventh to ninth centuries, and asserts a misguided though persistent doctrine of Byzantine feudalism. Many shorter histories of Byzantium have been published in recent years, but none has so far achieved the central position held by that of Ostrogorsky, nor do the current spate of handbooks and companions generally offer a comprehensive alternative analysis. Another traditional strategy among Byzantinists has been to seek to differentiate it from the medieval west. This insistence on Byzantine exceptionalism has been resisted, for example, by Judith Herrin, but when the late Evelyne Patlagean argued against it in her last book,[37] the book's reception demonstrated the tenacity of existing attitudes. But older views of the "crisis" of the eleventh century were already challenged by Paul Lemerle in the 1970s, and though Byzantium still lags far behind the Roman empire and indeed late antiquity in relation to the amount of archaeological data available, the results of archaeological work are nevertheless enabling a better understanding of issues on which former discussion was necessarily limited to reliance on textual evidence.[38]

Understanding the economic life of Byzantium implies understanding its trade and trading networks, and much more is now known about the changing nature of trading patterns. In its middle period Byzantium was part of a complex mesh of sea trade between the west, the northern regions, and especially the north and northeast coast of the Black Sea, Egypt, and the rest of the Muslim world.[39] Nevertheless, trade is only part of the story. The three-volume *Economic History of Byzantium* published in 2002 also illustrates the advances made in fields including the study of Byzantine numismatics, seals (once attached to documents that have themselves perished, and indicating the identity of officials and their positions), and archaeological investigation.[40] In particular, the surviving corpus of more than 75,000 official seals, albeit dispersed in individual collections, provide a vast mass of detailed information about persons, careers, and administrative organization.[41] The extent to which the early Byzantine economy was market-oriented is a subject that is currently arousing intense debate as part of a wider divide between primitivists and anti-primitivists in terms of the methodological understanding of the economy,[42] and much more needs to be done. A better understanding of the actual working of the Byzantine economy at all periods is the essential underpinning for serious consideration of the social macrostructures of Byzantium and its role and capacity as an empire.

Finally, Byzantium retained an imperial center throughout its history, doggedly holding onto it in exile after 1204. Members of the Palaeologan elite involved themselves in trading and financial alliances with Italians and others to an extent that might seem to have undermined the coherence of the Byzantine state. Yet the status of the imperial role was still upheld, even through usurpations and civil war (figure 4). It was maintained throughout the history of Byzantium by elaborate rituals, almost invariably with religious overtones and content, by a persistent and high-profile imperial rhetoric, and by a strong political and religious ideology that was continually being reinforced. The Byzantine emperors were masters of the populist theater of empire. Even the races and shows in the Hippodrome, traditionally condemned by the Fathers, came to be part of an imperial calendar dominated by the Christian year: "by the ninth to tenth centuries, the ceremonial of the Hippodrome was so visibly Christian that it resembled a solemn mass."[43] The culture of Byzantium was built around this daily performance of imperial power, without which it could not exist. Thus the prestige of the imperial office survived throughout the history of Byzantium, despite a high degree of challenge and instability, with frequent coups and sometimes even civil war.

Not surprising, then, if the emperor Constantine VII Porphyrogenitus, "born in the purple," whose own path to rule had not been

Figure 4. Jousting was also a favorite pursuit in Middle Byzantine court circles; This tenth-century ivory depicts two armed combatants. In 1159 the emperor Manuel I Comnenus (1118–80) himself took part in a famous tournament against crusader knights outside Antioch. ▪ Double sided comb depicting a jousting scene (ivory), Byzantine (10th century) / Germanisches Nationalmuseum, Nuremberg (Nuernberg), Germany / The Bridgeman Art Library

straightforward, laid such emphasis on the virtues of *taxis* ("order") in the preface to his *Book of Ceremonies.* Respect for order was constantly asserted in Byzantium, and all the more so when the actuality was frequent change, usurpation, and dynastic instability. In the last period of Byzantium, given the weakness of the Palaeologan state and its vulnerability to the encroaching Ottomans (to whom

Byzantium had spells of actual vassalage), this challenge was especially acute, and we can observe the patriarchs of this period taking the opportunity to proclaim a very high doctrine of their own authority. To describe Byzantium as totalitarian, with Alexander Kazhdan, is to miss the extent of these challenges and fail to recognize that emperor and church (especially emperor and patriarch) were often diametrically opposed to each other (see chapter 5). Orthodoxy constituted an important part of the apparatus of government and was a powerful tool for the emperors, and the church; its leading personages were an integral part of the state in a way that contrasts with the situation in the west (and perhaps accounts for the passionate opposition in Byzantium to the concept of papal primacy). But when emperors tried to force through their own religious agendas they were likely to encounter fierce and continued opposition.[44]

Nor, unlike the west, and despite the harsh rhetoric of condemnation in religious matters, which was often useful as a means of obscuring the extent of real opposition, was Byzantium a persecuting society. Its lawcodes allowed punishments involving mutilation that seem barbaric today, but capital punishment was rare (exile, not usually very severe, or deposition, were more common).[45] Books were burned in Byzantium (another legacy from the later Roman empire), but in this medieval society people usually survived.

Despite the many changes over its history, the imperial reach of Byzantium was wide, stretching all around the Mediterranean, to the east and the Islamic world, and to the north and to the Caucasus. Its rule and its influence were exercised militarily, diplomatically, politically, and economically. It was regarded in the west with a grudging admiration, and respected for the length of its traditions and its Roman past.

This was also a state that, however improbably, was able to absorb and survive a high degree of internal and external challenge over a period lasting many centuries. How this was achieved, and how Byzantium did in fact maintain itself as an empire are questions that still need to be asked.

CHAPTER 3

Hellenism

Who owns Byzantium? Is there a Byzantine identity?

Many would answer the last question in terms of its Christian Orthodoxy, others in terms of Hellenism, and therefore Greekness. As I shall argue here, the latter also necessarily engages—positively or negatively—with a persistent idea of Byzantium as a repository of Christianized Hellenism.

In recent years several Byzantinists have put forward the view of the Byzantine empire as a mélange of many peoples and cultures, its composition varying over time with the changing shape of the empire itself (chapters 1 and 2). Others, Cyril Mango among them, stress the Judeo-Christian and popular sides of the Byzantine mentality, in contrast with the traditional emphases on its classical elements and its high literary and intellectual culture.[1] A further group of scholars resists the stress laid in traditional Byzantine studies on continuity with the classical past and on elite culture by focusing on such themes as "daily life," the secular side of Byzantine life, economic activity and trade, the lower classes, and material culture.

However, the interpretation of Byzantium is especially fraught for Greek scholars. One of the most contentious aspects of this problem is the question of historical continuity, especially as it has been posed in relation to the modern Greek state. This chapter will be concerned in particular with the issue of Hellenism as seen against this context.

The reception of Byzantium in the new Greek state in the nineteenth century was both emotive and contested.[2] The liberated Greeks looked back to what they saw as their glorious classical past, and the notorious claim of the historian Jakob Fallmerayer that their past was not Greek but Slav met with heated opposition. The Byzantine phase of the history of Greece, identified by many with its Orthodox religion, resisted assimilation into the new national ideology, which sought to detach itself from the recent Ottoman past and to distinguish Greece as sharply as possible from the surviving Ottoman empire. But again there were opposing views, and this too gave rise to passionate feelings. By the end of the century, however, in the midst of a growing sense of Ottoman decline, Greek nationalism had combined with irredentism. This was to fail dramatically, after the ill-fated Greek landings in Asia Minor in 1919 and the Smyrna disaster of 1922, followed by the enforced exchange of Greek and Turkish populations. With the establishment of the Republic of Turkey, the recovery of Constantinople, the greatest prize for the Greeks, was out of reach.

The idea of Constantinople/Istanbul as the capital of a modern Greek state may seem counterintuitive today.[3] The "great idea" (as this ambition was termed by the Greeks themselves) also conflates two conceptions of Byzantium: as the seat of Orthodoxy and as an imperial power, a conflation that Peter Mackridge has warned against in a recent paper.[4] Yet Byzantium still occupies a privileged place in the consciousness of many Greeks. Nor, given the role of Greek as the language of government and culture throughout the history of Byzantium, the dependence of its educational system on classical Greek literature and rhetoric, and the ambivalence of Byzantine attitudes to ancient Greek philosophy, is it surprising to find that "Hellenism" is as fraught a concept within Byzantine studies as the Byzantine tradition is to Greeks today.

National traditions in Byzantine scholarship are not confined to Greece. With the beginnings of the academic discipline of Byzantine studies in the late nineteenth century, powerful academic traditions came into being in Tsarist Russia, Serbia, and Bulgaria—all Orthodox countries, and part of the "commonwealth" discussed in the preceding chapter. The role of Byzantium in these countries and in southeastern Europe generally (often expressed in terms of its "legacy") is also complex. Byzantine studies also developed in some European centers, notably Paris and Vienna, and in Germany, alongside the editing and publication of Byzantine texts.[5] This did not happen in the same way in the Anglo-Saxon world, where the rare scholars who did venture into the Byzantine period were usually classicists by origin. In a later generation, Steven Runciman was an exception to this generalization, having studied history at Cambridge. His teacher J. B. Bury, whose only pupil at Cambridge was Runciman, had held chairs of Greek and History simultaneously at Trinity College Dublin, and had published on classical

Greek as well as Byzantine history. Younger British Byzantinists complain of this heritage, which has certainly led to some very negative judgments of Byzantium and Byzantine literature when compared with that of classical Greece. A notorious example is the 1963 article on Byzantine literature by Romilly Jenkins, also a classicist, who held the Koraes Chair of Modern Greek and Byzantine History, Language and Literature at King's College London from 1946 to 1960,[6] and was simultaneously Honorary Lecturer in Classical Archaeology in the College. Jenkins warned that Byzantine literature was not a mere offshoot of classical antiquity but "an independent entity, created out of a fusion of Greek, Roman, oriental and native Byzantine elements."[7] This was not meant to be complimentary. He went on to complain of its tediousness and to state that it is hardly possible to recall a line from the "reams of iambic verses" produced by Byzantium's "best" writers and scholars. He also writes of "the total lack of poetic feeling and appreciation at Byzantium during the most cultured epoch of her renaissance." Jenkins's grudging conclusion is also worth citing: "Let us be grateful that the mediaeval Byzantine adhered with fidelity to at least some of the traditions handed down from a world more liberally minded and more cultivated than his own."

Byzantium has been caught between the hostile, or at least prejudiced, assumptions of some classically trained scholars and the national and the religious agendas of Greek and other Orthodox writers. To Mackridge again, "Classical Athens has been nationalized in modern Greece . . . Byzantium has been similarly nationalized," the latter representing the medieval phase of Hellenism.[8] At the heart of this view of Byzantium is the vexed question of the continuity (or lack of it) of Greek civilization (figure 5). This is a problem only too well recognized among Greek Byzantinists, and even if Greek scholarship in the past has tended to assume continuity, opinions vary much more than these quotations suggest.[9] The awkward relation of the modern Greek state with the monasteries of Mount Athos, with their very diverse monastic population, is a further indicator of the emotion that still surrounds the issue.

"Hellenism" (a term whose uses I will discuss further later) also goes far beyond the nation state of modern Greece. The Byzantine state was never coterminous with Greece, even in the Palaeologan period, when there were minor statelets in Epirus and the Morea and an enclave at Mistra.[10] The contested period of Slav settlement characterized the late sixth and seventh centuries in Greece, and despite the establishment of a "theme" (military and administrative organization) of "Hellas," Byzantine control was uncertain and insecure before the successful imperial initiatives of the late ninth and tenth centuries.[11] It was not only the "missions to the Slavs" that extended Byzantium's reach far beyond Greece and Asia Minor.[12] In addition to the countries of the "Byzantine commonwealth," Hellenism also left a continuing imprint on the Middle East, even after the rise of Islam. We read constantly of the transmission of Greek culture to Baghdad from Alexandria. But Greek language and culture were rooted in the whole of the eastern Mediterranean, and this was not the only route by which they passed into

Figure 5. The Parthenon in Athens, used as a church of the Virgin in the medieval period (its traces were later removed). ▪ Image © Ivan Bastien / shutterstock.com

Arabic. The language of government and culture in the eastern Roman empire had long been Greek, and Greek language and culture long continued to be important in the east despite an active Greek into Syriac translation movement in late antiquity.[13] In the early seventh century Sophronius, the patriarch of Jerusalem, who according to tradition handed over the city to the caliph Umar, had received a classical training in Damascus. At the same time an astonishing amount of classicizing iconography continued to be displayed in the mosaics that continued to be laid in churches in what is now Jordan even in the late Umayyad period, long after Byzantine rule in the region had ended.[14]

How useful, then, is the concept of Hellenism in trying to understand Byzantine identity?

As has often been pointed out, the Byzantines thought of themselves as Romans, and their empire as the Roman empire. In the earlier Christian centuries the term "Hellene" or "Hellenic" had been appropriated in Greek by Christian writers to refer to pagans, and thus acquired a very negative connotation.[15] Many generations of churchmen accordingly condemned Hellenic philosophy, and when the philosopher John Italus ("the Italian," because he came from Calabria in southern Italy) was condemned as a heretic under the emperor Alexius I Comnenus in 1082, the charges included his alleged resort to Hellenic ideas, and the claim that he "believed" in the doctrines of Plato rather than simply reading his works as literature. Only in the period of the enforced engagement with the west that came with the Crusades (which also began during the reign of Alexius), the assertiveness of the papacy, and the theological debates with the Latins, when "Rome" seemed to have taken on a new meaning, did the Byzantines begin to use the term "Hellenes" to refer to themselves; we also encounter the term *Graikos*, used by Latins but also applied to the Orthodox (or Byzantine) spokesman in some Greek texts of these theological debates, and adopted even in official contexts.[16]

In *Roumeli*, his book about northern Greece, the travel-writer Patrick Leigh Fermor writes of the "Helleno-Romaic dilemma." He even drew up a list of the supposedly contrasting characteristics that he claimed existed within every Greek (some admittedly "purposely slight and frivolous," but included for better illustrative effect).[17] This should not be dismissed as merely a literary construction; indeed another recent article talks of "two Greeces." The problem, however, lies with understanding what is meant by "Greek" and still more by "Hellenic."

A major difficulty lies with the slippery nature of the very term "Hellenism," a word that carries heavy baggage. Leaving aside here the use of concepts such as "Hellenic" and "barbarian" in the classical period, references to "Hellenism" have been central in discussions of early Christianity in terms of a supposed opposition between Jewish origins and Greek philosophical thought. The famous lecture given by Pope Benedict XVI in Regensburg in 2006 was titled "Faith, Reason and the University: Memories and Reflections" and was in fact a justification of this understanding of Hellenism as a basic feature of Christianity.[18] Although Rowan Williams once wrote that "There is no possibility of de-Hellenizing Christian dogma, because that would be a refusal to accept what history means," this perceived opposition was an issue with which many early Christian writers also struggled.[19] It has given rise to a huge secondary literature on early Christian and Jewish identity and a sophisticated theoretical approach to the issue, in which Hellenism is viewed by some scholars as a process, or even a theoretical "toolbox" for historians trying to understand the cultural and religious changes taking place in the Roman empire and in late antiquity.[20]

"Hellenism" is also used to denote the intellectual and cultural tradition of Greek literature and philosophy in the Roman empire. In particular, the emperor Julian's attempt to reverse the hold of Christianity in the empire during his brief reign (361–63) is commonly couched in terms of Hellenism.[21] The term is also commonly used instead of "classical" in discussions of the education and culture of Christian patristic writers such as Gregory of Nazianzus: Christian intellectuals and writers had a schizophrenic relation to classical culture and aspired to and sought to appropriate and exploit Greek *paideia* while at the same time condemning it.[22] A genealogical theory of Christian origins also developed, in which Christians were constructed as "the third race," and indeed, in what may now strike the reader as strange, the late-fourth-century heresiologist Epiphanius of Salamis lists Hellenism alongside Barbarism, Scythism, and Judaism as one of the original sects from which all other heresies have sprung. Epiphanius was elaborating on the four categories mentioned at Colossians 3:11 and Galatians 3:28 (and he was not the first to do so). But as we have also seen, "Hellenism" can also be applied in a more general way to mythological and other classicizing themes in the art and literature of late antiquity. Indeed, given the influence exerted on Byzantine literature by the Greek writers of the Second Sophistic movement of the second and third centuries, and the value placed by intellectuals in Byzantium on the imitation of the classical and later Greek authors (chapter 1), Hellenism in this sense was inscribed in Byzantine elite culture itself.

None of these usages carries the sense of national, ethnic, or territorial continuity with classical Greece. But a recent book by Anthony Kaldellis demonstrates the dilemmas faced by Greek historians in writing about Byzantium.[23] Kaldellis, a Greek himself, explicitly distances himself from modern Greek and Greek-American scholarship on Byzantium, with what he calls its "casual equation of Greeks and Byzantines,"[24] by constructing the Byzantines as "Romans" in a way that might have surprised them had they heard it. This move allows him to detach the concept of Hellenism from the generally assumed Orthodox identity of Byzantium, despite the fact that educated Byzantines themselves wrote in highly literary Greek and hardly knew Latin writings until Augustine was translated along with Aquinas, as described in chapter 1. (Kaldellis ends his book at 1261, when the Byzantines returned to Constantinople.) After emphasising that the Byzantines called themselves Romans, and arguing that Byzantium was not a multiethnic empire but "the nation state of the Romans," he discusses three phases of "Hellenism": late antiquity, the age of Michael Psellus (eleventh century), and the Comnenian period (late eleventh and twelfth centuries). Between the first and second, from about 400 to 1040, comes a period he calls "Hellenism in limbo," when, he claims, Hellenic culture went into abeyance.

In other publications dealing with the historians Procopius and Agathias and their contemporary John Lydus, and with Michael Psellus, Kaldellis has also argued for Neoplatonic and "Hellenic" agendas.[25] If with Kaldellis we understand Hellenism in Byzantium not merely as referring to high literary culture but also as carrying overtones of rationalism and secret opposition, and if Byzantium itself is constructed as a Roman state, rather than an Orthodox empire, the notion of Orthodoxy as the defining characteristic of Byzantium is deconstructed, and Byzantium can be reclaimed for the cause of rationalism and dissent. Not surprisingly, Kaldellis includes among his targets the notion of a Byzantine commonwealth underpinned by a concept of universalism with Orthodoxy as one of the main features holding it together.

Kaldellis's book vividly reveals the dilemmas that present themselves to scholars of Greek origin when writing about Byzantium. The agenda of an underlying—and supposedly continuous—strand of oppositional rationalism (defined as Hellenism) has been taken considerably further by another Greek scholar, Niketas Siniossoglou, in a recent book about George Gemistus Plethon,[26] to which I will return shortly. Last, a distaste for Orthodox Byzantium, combined with, or rather, arising from, a high valuation of late antique Neoplatonism, can also be detected in recent publications by Polymnia Athanassiadi (chapter 2).[27]

According to Kaldellis, Hellenism in Byzantium, as in late antiquity, was constructed and changing. This is an approach with which we can agree. But here again we meet the problem for Byzantinists highlighted in chapter 1 and posed by the huge changes that have taken place in the study of late antiquity in the last generation. The view of a Byzantine historian looking back on the earlier centuries from the later perspective is different from that of a late antique scholar who is doing just the opposite—pushing his or her subject ever further forward chronologically and more to the east geographically. In general, historians of late antiquity also display a much more developed theoretical approach to cultural and religious change than is as yet apparent in the field of Byzantine studies.[28] The difficult subject of Greek identity in Byzantium, whether or not to be identified with Hellenism, immediately raises questions of periodization and geographical coverage—when did "Byzantium" begin, and how distinct was it from "late antiquity"? If the "long" Byzantium is adopted, there has to be engagement with the vast scholarship on late antiquity in its present form, including its discussion of Hellenism. To expose and react to the dilemmas in existing Greek scholarship on Byzantium will not be sufficient.[29]

It perhaps does not matter much whether Byzantium is deemed to have begun with Constantine or only later, except that Byzantine historians have to deal with the fact that the roots of many (admittedly of course not all) features of later Byzantine culture and society lie in an earlier period. In that period, which in current scholarship is often called late antiquity rather than early Byzantium,[30] intense and sometimes exciting cultural and religious change went alongside momentous political and military developments. Christianity, in whatever form, did become dominant in the empire run from Constantinople, but a new world religion—namely, Islam—was also born in the context of the "Byzantine" or late antique eastern Mediterranean. "Greek" or "Hellenic" identities were negotiated not only in relation to Roman but also to eastern ones; the emergence of "Arab" identities is one of the most debated issues in current scholarship. The Roman law school in Beirut used Latin for its teaching, but the Christian rhetors of late antique Gaza wrote in high-style Greek, and Sophronius, the patriarch of Jerusalem mentioned earlier, constructed Hellenism as the deceptive antithesis of the power of the saints in his collection of miracle stories associated with the shrine of saints Cyrus and John in Egypt, even while composing Greek classicizing anacreontic poems on contemporary events.[31]

Discussion of "Hellenism," or of Greek identity in early Byzantium, cannot be confined to Constantinople and its heartlands, or indeed to Greece itself. Neoplatonic philosophy continued to be practiced in the Academy at Athens until the emperor Justinian's measures against it in AD 529, and Alexandria remained a center of philosophical teaching thereafter, while the Athenian philosophers themselves found ways of carrying on their writing. North Africa, Egypt, and the eastern Mediterranean were still governed by Constantinople until the Persian and Arab invasions, and the impact of Byzantine practices continued. In Italy, too, the Greek influence in Rome, as well as in Sicily and southern Italy, received new and important impetus in the seventh and eighth centuries, presenting further issues of identity.

Scholarship on late antiquity in the last generation has refined and applied theoretical models for the discussion of identity formation in an impressive way to subjects including late antique Judaism, religious identities in Antioch, the uses of Greek and Syriac in ecclesiastical contexts, and the emergence of Arab identity.[32] This builds on an equally extensive literature on identity and ethnicity in the classical period, and on revisionist approaches on such older themes as "Romanization" in the imperial period. Concepts such as "hybridity," borrowed from postcolonialist criticism, and of identities as shifting, constructed, and often multiple, which lie behind this work, have barely as yet been applied to Byzantium.[33]

The discursive construction of identity (and of "Hellenism") needs to be brought into much greater prominence with regard to Byzantium. This is not easy when, as suggested in chapter 1, so much still needs to be done. The analysis of Byzantine literature, the key carrier of the classical Greek tradition in Byzantium, is central to issues of identity and Hellenism. That the method of New Historicism, the product of the 1980s, is only now being applied by some as a tool for the study of Byzantine literature tells us something itself about this time lag, and while Byzantine texts certainly do call for the kind of contextual approach found in the work of Stephen Greenblatt, Byzantine historians would also do well to look more to discourse analysis and to language and writing as mechanisms of identity and power. I will reserve until chapter 5 remarks on Byzantine theological writing, which perhaps poses the greatest challenge to historians and indeed to literary scholars who are not themselves theologians, but which is central to the issues discussed in this chapter.

But neither Hellenism nor identity are simply a matter of texts. Archaeologists and art historians of other periods have been much exercised about the degree of emphasis that should be given to the active influence of material culture in forming cultural consciousness.[34] At the same time evidence from archaeology and material culture has become central to scholarship on late antiquity, including discussions of identity and cultural differentiation. The same needs to happen with the history of Byzantium.[35]

As I mentioned earlier, Anthony Kaldellis himself puts forward the view that Hellenic identity is discursively constructed; similarly, "'Hellenism and Christianity' was a constructed opposition, constantly negotiated and variously represented."[36] But the field of negotiation he envisages for the early Byzantine or late antique period is limited, focusing on high culture, the field of Greek *paideia*: "The majority of Byzantines did not worry about Hellenism one way or the other."[37] But texts are not innocent, especially in matters of identity. Byzantine discourse was powerfully prescriptive, creating identity and proscribing difference. Nowhere is this more apparent than in theological and religious discourse, but it also applies in other fields, and provides a continuing context for the competitive literary and intellectual engagement by which elite Byzantines furthered their life chances. Naturally we also see it in political and public discourse, and a rhetorical analysis of Byzantine imperial pronouncements, for example, would be one of the best ways of countering the positivist readings that prevail even now in Byzantine scholarship.

In his book *Radical Platonism*, Niketas Siniossoglou takes the late Byzantine Hellenism of Gemistos Plethon as the starting point

Figure 6. The ruins of Mistra in the Peloponnese, seat of a Byzantine court and intense intellectual life in the late Byzantine period, especially associated with George Gemistos Plethon, to whose circle the future Cardinal Bessarion also belonged. ▪ Image © Roger Wood / CORBIS

for an interpretation of Hellenism in Byzantium in which he adopts a very different approach. One of the leading Byzantine intellectuals of the early fifteenth century, and a member of the court at Mistra in the Peloponnese (figure 6), Plethon was a prolific writer whose Platonizing views, expressed especially in his *Laws*, attracted the condemnation of George Gennadius Scholarius and have long intrigued modern scholars.[38] For Siniossoglou, Plethon's work represents the clearest manifestation of a Platonizing paganism that he sees as a constant thread running throughout Byzantine history. Siniossoglou is an advocate of a philosophical essentialism based on Weberian ideal-types, the very opposite of the discursive anti-essentialism discussed earlier. He is interested in "the modalities and tropes through which a Platonist worldview antagonistic to Christianity was preserved, appropriated, recalibrated and continuously juxtaposed to Christian monastic and clerical hegemony."[39] In this formulation, Plethon's views were a direct challenge to the idea of Roman and Orthodox identity in Byzantium, and for Siniossoglou this was no mere aberration, but the logical culmination of a continuous previous tradition.

The ground for this interpretation was prepared in an earlier book by the same author on the fifth-century writer Theodoret of Cyrrhus, where Siniossoglou argues for Hellenism and Christianity as different in essence, "separate intellectual entities," "neither artificial nor socially constructed."[40] The common idea of "Christian Hellenism"—that is, the genuine appropriation of Hellenic concepts within a Christian and Orthodox worldview, over and above mere terminology, is for him an impossibility. Like Kaldellis, Siniossoglou detaches Hellenism from Christianity, and in particular from Orthodoxy. He addresses the question of continuity ("the essential continuity between the Hellenes and us") directly, and denies the idea of a Greek continuity through "Christian Hellenism" and Byzantine Orthodoxy.[41] His deliberate preference for the term "Roman Orthodoxy" makes the point even clearer.

Writing on Plethon, at the end of the Byzantine period, Siniossoglou argues for an "awakening" of philosophical Hellenism on the eve of the Turkish conquest that can be read as the key to Spinoza and to modernity.[42] Plethon wrote in a context of deep anxiety and division about the present and future of Greek culture in the face of competing pressure exerted by Italy on the one hand and the Ottomans on the other. Within Byzantium itself an intense debate about the respective importance of Plato and Aristotle also served as the context for Plethon's position, as well as a partial surrogate for the anxieties surrounding Greek and Orthodox identity.[43] He himself had given lectures in Florence in 1439 on the differences between Plato and Aristotle,[44] attacking the latter; they were followed by a reply from Scholarius and a further justification from Plethon himself.

Some difficulties have to be overcome in order to present Plethon's revived Platonic philosophy in this way. Prominent among them is the awkward fact that not only was he himself included in the large Byzantine delegation that supported the emperor John VIII Palaeologus at the Council of Ferrara/Florence in 1438–39 but he also composed a treatise against Latin theology. At least one contemporary regarded him as a sincere defender of the Orthodox position.[45] Not surprisingly, this has puzzled many scholars. Either it was necessary for him to dissemble, as Siniossoglou believes, or his Hellenism was not as radical as it might appear. According to C. M. Woodhouse it was Plethon's drafting skills rather than his Orthodox credentials that were needed at the council; Woodhouse further argued that like Psellus and Italus, Plethon valued philosophy over theology. There were also many tempting opportunities in Italy for Byzantine intellectuals conscious of the dire situation of Constantinople.[46] Nor was Plethon the only contemporary for whom in the last days of Byzantium the question of Hellenic identity presented itself in an acute form.[47]

Plethon died at a great age soon after the fall of Constantinople, a highly controversial figure in his own time.[48] Scholarius obtained a copy of Plethon's treatise modeled on Plato's *Laws* from the Despina Theodora of the Morea and ordered it to be burned along with any other remaining copies. It is hard to know where the truth lies about Plethon's allegiances, but it is clear enough that Siniossoglou's hypothesis of a continuous Platonizing opposition as the carrier of Hellenic identity within Byzantium has a clear Greek and anti-Orthodox agenda, and depends, as we saw, on a strongly essentialist way of looking at identity.[49]

However, identity is also a matter of self-representation. While the Byzantines who defined themselves as "Christian" or "Orthodox" were adopting a religious marker, this was not the only way in which they distinguished themselves; further, as we shall see in chapter 5, the term "Orthodox" also caused deep internal divisions. Sustained challenge and redefinition constitute a more promising model for Byzantine identity than either successful appropriation on the one hand or existential opposition on the other. From the perspective of Christianity, Hellenism remained a difficult concept:

"cette Grèce problématique que l'on ne peut jamais totalement s'approprier."[50] Some memories of ancient Greek wisdom passed into the realm of legend,[51] and for all the classical manuscripts and editing of classical texts with which Palaeologan intellectuals were engaged, and the genuine depth of classical learning in later Byzantium, the Greece so eagerly rediscovered by the west during the Renaissance had a novelty and freshness that were by definition unknown to Byzantium.

In a well-known essay of 1975, the eminent Greek Byzantinist Hélène Ahrweiler suggested that the universalism that Byzantium had inherited from the Roman empire in its early period gave way from the eighth century onward to an aggressive nationalism based on Greek and Orthodox patriotism. More recently, and in a different context, she discussed the difficult question of Hellenism and Greek continuity, with full awareness of the complications of the Byzantine period, now cautiously suggesting that "Helleno-centric Christianity, that is, Orthodoxy" did indeed represent the continuance of ancient Greek humanism, and emphasizing the fact that classical Greece extended beyond the territorial base of Greece itself.[52] But again, during most of their history the Byzantines did not self-identify as Hellenes; again, it could be argued, in contrast, that one of the very strengths of Byzantium was its flexibility and the capacity of its people to look in several directions.

Kaldellis's view is rather different: for him Byzantium represents the "nation-state of the Romans," rather than of the Greeks. But the concept of an emerging nation state is not helpful in this case; nor were the "Byzantines" a new people who underwent the process of ethnogenesis posited for the peoples of the early medieval west.[53] They continued to call themselves Romans because the origins of Byzantium lay in the eastern Roman empire; their majority as well as their high-style literary and administrative language was Greek, because that was also the language of the eastern part of the late Roman empire.[54] Their educational system was overwhelmingly based on Greek models, Greek rhetorical handbooks, and, for some, the philosophy of Plato and Aristotle, but this too was a direct inheritance from the eastern Roman empire, where Greek language and culture already flourished under the framework of Roman rule long before the foundation of Constantinople. The "Second Sophistic," whose authors were so important in the Byzantine literary tradition, was itself a movement born in the Roman imperial period.[55] Moreover, the Fathers to whom Byzantine theologians constantly appealed were themselves the Greek theologians who wrote in the context of the Roman empire; few if any Latin theological writers were commonly cited in theological literature until late in Byzantium's history. In order to make sense of Byzantine identity, or Hellenism in Byzantium, we need to start not merely from late antiquity, but from this earlier period of the Roman empire and Roman imperial rule in the east.

Nor, whatever identity might be claimed for Byzantium, was it based on ethnicity. Even if Byzantium was not quite the multiethnic empire that some would like it to have been, the population of its core provinces was thoroughly mixed. Cyril Mango's robust characterization of the situation in the late eighth century conveys the idea very vividly: "We find a population that had been so thoroughly churned up that it is difficult to tell what ethnic groups were living where and in what numbers."[56] We see vividly illustrated in the tenth-century *De administrando imperio* of the emperor Constantine VII Porphyrogenitus that Byzantium was surrounded by emerging peoples with evolving identities. Hybridity was built into the very nature of Byzantium and so were the multiple identities so familiar to its varying population and the different phases of its history. Byzantine identity was not only Greek: Byzantium is for all. "Hellenism" was important, but it is not enough.

CHAPTER 4

The Realms of Gold

> The fiery vision of the radiant icon simulates in its glittering both the radiant Mother of God and the fiery hour of the Last Judgement.
>
> —B. V. Pentcheva

> Byzantine tactile visuality rested on an aesthetic of exuberant surfaces. These present a taste for sensual pleasure stimulated by an abundance of textures, glittering light effects, the sweetness of honey and incense, and sound.
>
> —B. V. Pentcheva[1]

These statements, albeit from a highly technical book, do something to convey a common reaction on first acquaintance with Byzantine art. It was Byzantine art that fascinated travelers like Robert Byron and Thomas Whittemore in the early twentieth century (chapter 1), and drew them to the civilization from which it came. In Britain artists from the Royal Academy of Arts were associated with the British School at Athens (founded in 1886), and set about recording and drawing Byzantine buildings. The discovery of Byzantium by the Arts and Crafts movement was very much of the period too.[2] Walter George, who drew the basilica of St. Demetrius in Thessalonike for the British School at Athens before the great fire of 1917, was taught at the Royal College of Art by the architect and scholar William Lethaby, famous to Byzantinists for his work on Hagia Sophia in Constantinople. In the Ottoman period and until the mid-nineteenth century the mosaics inside Hagia Sophia were plastered over, and after they had been uncovered, restored, and recorded by the Fossati brothers and by W. Salzenburg in the 1850s they had had to be plastered over again.[3] Hagia Sophia was still a mosque when the American art historian Thomas Whittemore's good relationship with Ataturk allowed work to begin on the conservation of the mosaics in 1931. The building was secularized soon after and the work continued for nearly two decades. In 1930 Whittemore had founded the Byzantine Institute of America, initially in Boston but with outposts in Paris and Istanbul, and its work was eventually absorbed into the Byzantine research center at Dumbarton Oaks in Washington, DC. The historic study and restoration of the frescoes and mosaics of the Chora monastery (the Kariye Camii), also in Istanbul, was the result of a collaboration between the Institute and Dumbarton Oaks.

Edwin Freshfield (d. 1918), of the British legal family, was another antiquarian and traveler in the Levant, with a wife who had Smyrna connections. He chaired the Byzantine Research Fund at the British School in Athens, and his son, Edwin Hanson Freshfield (d. 1948), was a student of Byzantine law and yet another Levantine traveler. In 1903 Westminster Cathedral in London was completed, designed in Byzantine style ("cheaper than Gothic").[4] Co-secretary of the Byzantine Research Fund was O. M. Dalton of the British

Museum, whose own book on Byzantine art and archaeology was published in 1911; it is typical of the period that he saw Byzantium's greatest achievement as lying in its mosaics, architecture, painting, and minor arts.[5]

Aesthetic responses were central to this discovery of Byzantine art and architecture. Whittemore was a figure who also attracted the attention of writers, including Edith Wharton and Evelyn Waugh, and Robert Byron belonged to the same set as Evelyn Waugh at Oxford in the 1920s, where they were both members of the notorious but harmless Hypocrites Club.[6] What Byron hoped for in *The Byzantine Achievement* was to "quicken the historical emotion" of the reader, "when next obtrudes on his notice the seaboard of the Greeks and its capital city of Constantinople."[7] He had an idealized view of Byzantine art that would certainly not satisfy art historians today—his approach was alternately naïve and patronizing, and his points of comparison derived from his own recent experience as an undergraduate at Oxford. Of the monasteries of Mount Athos, he thought, you could study in both date and plan the "exact counterparts of English university colleges," without the "meanness" of later Gothic.[8] For Byron, too, as for others in this early period, the aesthetic appeal of Byzantine art was an important element in the enthusiasm with which it was greeted.

Not all Byzantine art was a luxury art. However, the lasting appeal of its use of gold, silver, enamel, and precious stones is also evident from the choice of objects in blockbuster exhibitions and in the admiring reactions of their visitors (figure 7).[9] The latter represent a response to Byzantine art and architecture that also found expression among the Byzantines themselves, who composed many lengthy and detailed literary descriptions (*ekphraseis*) of art works or buildings. Light and color, as well as gold and glitter, are key features in these works, and light is the dominant feature in the description of the newly built Justinianic Hagia Sophia by Procopius of Caesarea—when Byzantines described marble, what they emphasized was its sheen and brilliance.[10]

A high proportion of surviving Byzantine art is religious. This does not mean that the Byzantines were all religious themselves; rather, it tells us about patronage and how art was commissioned.[11] Impressive silverware and ivory objects remain from the late antique period, some of them clearly commissioned by the wealthy elite,[12] though the members of the later Byzantine aristocracy were more likely to commission an illustrated psalter or found a church or a monastery. Among the finest examples of late Byzantine art are the frescoes and mosaics commissioned for the Chora monastery in Constantinople already mentioned, by the early fourteenth-century writer, statesman, and courtier Theodore Metochites. But of the many glittering examples of luxury religious art from Byzantium, the extraordinary treasures looted by the Fourth Crusade in 1204 and now in San Marco, Venice, are hard to match, as was clear from the reaction when they were included in the winter of 2008–9 in a major Byzantine exhibition at the Royal Academy in London. Many visitors found them hard to understand, but nearly all found them breathtaking. One can easily understand why some Byzan-

Figure 7. A gleaming icon: St. Michael, tenth century, now in the Treasury of St. Mark's, Venice. ▪ Photograph © Hirmer Fotoarchiv München. Reproduced with the permission of the Basilica di San Marco, Venice

tinists, including some art historians, wish to distance themselves from such an approach.

In the words of Gilbert Dagron, "Byzance n'entre pas aisément dans les schémas d'une histoire de l'art ordinaire [Byzantium does not fit easily into the categories of conventional art history]."[13] Byzantine art presents problems for modern audiences and modern interpreters alike, and we need to ask what this apparent exceptionalism means.[14] The difficulty is compounded by the fact that contemporaries often praised the realism of objects when it is their very unfamiliarity and apparent stylization that many modern viewers find attractive. Nor is it clear that the terms the Byzantines used for color correspond easily with ours.[15] The Byzantines also developed a sophisticated theory of perception very different from our own. To a western eye their art seems formulaic and lacking in perspective; the famous early icon of St. Peter from the Monastery of St. Catherine on Mount Sinai has recently been described as "extraordinarily skilled" but also as "clearly two-dimensionalized," with "flatness" a "defining feature."[16] This "flatness" in Byzantine icons has commonly been seen as intensely spiritual.[17] In addition icons often presuppose a narrative or theological subject matter that has to be decoded before it can be understood. Last, the Byzantines themselves engaged in an intense debate about the relation between word and images, eventually resolved at the end of the iconoclastic controversy of the eighth and ninth centuries in favor of images, when the ninth-century declaration known as the *Synodikon of Orthodoxy* included the veneration of religious images as one of the markers of Orthodoxy. It is striking that the term "the triumph of Orthodoxy" was used to denote both the resolution of this struggle and the liturgical feast that was established to commemorate it (chapter 5).[18]

In a recent book Michael Squire explains what he sees as a strong contrast in modern attitudes to western medieval and Byzantine art in terms of the absence in Byzantium of the western legacy of the Protestant Reformation and its privileging of the written word.[19] In contrast, Byzantium not only declared images equal to texts but went even further and privileged the image, claiming that words could lie but images conveyed the truth. This was not an easy position to maintain. It involved explaining why neither the Scriptures nor the Fathers had expressed this doctrine (some had even opposed religious art); appeal had therefore to be made to the force of an "unwritten tradition." Arguments in the first phase of the quarrel over religious images in the eighth and early ninth centuries focused on the danger of idolatry and the difference between worship and mere veneration—a necessary precaution at a time when enthusiasm for religious images could easily lead to excess. Writing from the monastery of St. Sabas near Jerusalem, which was by then within the Umayyad caliphate, John of Damascus drew up an authoritative and cautionary set of guidelines. Church councils in 754 and 787 first condemned and then justified the veneration of religious images, marshaling a vast and ever-more sophisticated barrage of arguments and authorities. But the affair was not dead. Another council hostile to images followed in 815, and the defense of images became more technical and more philosophical, appealing to prototype and archetype and to sophisticated theories of representation.[20] The leading defenders of images in this period, Theodore, abbot of the Studios monastery in Constantinople, and the patriarch Nicephorus, were remembered later as the canonical heroes of official attitudes. They were depicted in icons showing the end of the controversy in 843 as the "triumph" of Orthodoxy, and when the issue was revived in the eleventh century (chapter 5; and see figure 9 later) they were the authorities to whom appeal was made.

In the case of Byzantium, in contrast with the west, the reaction against depicting the divine in art came early, and it failed. This failure, seen conversely by the Byzantines as the "triumph" of images, was celebrated in highly tendentious versions of the controversy produced by the successful iconophiles. Just how much they manipulated the narrative has been recognized in recent scholarship, and amounted at times to the deliberate fabrication and interpolation of texts.[21] The victory over iconoclasm was also illustrated visually, most famously in the illustrated psalter known as the "Khludov" psalter, which contains gloating depictions of the failed iconoclast attack on images.[22]

Influenced by the relatively recent recognition of the level of tendentiousness in the central contemporary texts, revisionist scholarship downplays the wider political and social impact of the "iconoclastic controversy."[23] Many bishops and monks were willing to change their positions, especially in its later stages. All was indeed not as it has seemed. But the lengthy debates and intensive literary production from the period ensured that a highly theoretical and self-conscious contemporary discourse developed in relation to Byzantine art. Anxiety about religious images was felt well before the "iconoclast era," which Leslie Brubaker has defined as beginning only in AD 680. How could saints be recognized? Were images of Christ true likenesses? These were questions Christians increasingly asked themselves in the sixth and seventh centuries, a period when they also questioned whether the saints really had power after their deaths. The latter anxiety has been highlighted recently by several scholars.[24] It was debated by contemporary authors in theological terms, and this spilled over into the debates about the status of religious images. One of the questioners in the seventh-century collection of "Questions and Answers" by Anastasius of Sinai suggested that it was angels, not the saints, who were responsible for visions of the saints in churches and at their tombs.[25] It was but a small step from appearances of the saints and the Virgin in dreams and visions to anxieties about their representations in visual art, or, conversely, to an appeal to visions as a means whereby the likenesses in icons could be verified.[26] Elsewhere the same Anastasius appealed to the visual as a means of verification of the real suffering of Christ on the cross, and to material signs in preference to texts, on the grounds that texts could be falsified.[27] Religious images also had an uncanny tendency to spawn copies of themselves: images of images of images. No wonder the risks from mistaken identity or impersonation were so high when the truth of visual likenesses was a matter of such deep concern.[28]

These anxieties built on still deeper fears. During the iconoclast and iconophile debates of the eighth and ninth centuries the supporters of images identified their enemies as "Jewish"-minded or "Saracen"-minded. The triumph of Orthodoxy in 843 was also proclaimed as the triumph of Christianity over Judaism, and this too was illustrated in visual art.[29] The intense arguments about images were accompanied by a virulent anti-Jewish tone in contemporary writing. John of Damascus's defence of religious images followed seamlessly on from a spate of Christian *Adversus Iudaeos* apologetic texts in which a detailed repertoire of arguments was deployed to counter the supposed Jewish accusation of idolatry. As created objects, religious images naturally took their place in the late seventh century alongside the wood of the cross and other examples within this anxious and hostile anti-Jewish discourse, in which appeal was made to the Old Testament for counterexamples of alleged idolatry on the part of the Jews: the ark, manna, the tablets of the Law. It also reflected an existing and much wider anti-Jewish tone in written texts.[30] Jews also feature in several of the contemporary tales told about miraculous images, and among the illustrations in the ninth-century Khludov psalter, carefully aligned with the appropriate Psalms, we find illustrations of Jews attacking the icon of Christ.[31] Taking together the surviving preiconoclastic texts and the posticonoclastic productions of the iconophiles, it is not hard to detect a steadily growing anxiety about the status of images. Iconophiles hoped and believed the arguments of the eighth and ninth centuries had put this to rest, but the extraordinary effort that they put into rewriting the record *post eventum* suggests that they still felt it necessary to make quite sure that this was the case.

The theorizing of likeness in Byzantium during and after the iconoclastic controversy took place within the specific context of religious images and their theological justification. But the interplay of word and image in Byzantium extended much more widely. The fact that Byzantines themselves often wrote about visual art or architecture, and the terms in which they did so, present special problems of interpretation: did they perceive art in the same way as we do now, and in the instances when we can compare textual and artistic representations, what is the relation between them? According to Leslie Brubaker, they are quite different: "words and images communicate differently: words describe, images show."[32] Not everyone agrees with this position, and the existence of an already large secondary literature suggests that there is something to explain. According to an alternative formulation, "Art and text, the interface between images and words, is one of the oldest issues in art history" and "the dynamic between art and text in Byzantium is essential for understanding Byzantine society, where the correct relationship between the two was critical to the well-being of the state."[33] In the same introduction, Liz James also says that "any discussion of art and text in Byzantine culture needs also to engage with the nature of Byzantine written sources as verbal," and asks whether art needs text.[34] It seems clear at any rate that art historians need texts and "text historians" need art history.

Much attention has been drawn to the way in which Byzantine visual art itself incorporates texts—often the names, or abbreviated names, of those depicted, but sometimes also longer texts. Why was it felt necessary to identify the subject matter, even when it might be thought to be obvious? Then there is the case of epigrams written about works of art, and finally, the many rhetorical descriptions of art works known as *ekphraseis*. Much has been written about all these, and I do not wish to add to it here.[35] How far do *ekphraseis* express the way in which Byzantine art was actually perceived, and what do they tell us about the viewer? There was nothing new in the Byzantine period about *ekphrasis*, the rhetorical description of works of art; it was a taste inherited from poetic models from the classical period and from the rhetorical practice of the Second Sophistic, which was so influential on Byzantine high-style literature. "Vividness," or *energeia*, was the touchstone of a successful rhetorical *ekphrasis*, achieved by stylistic means but also connected with an understanding of perception set out in the third-century *Eikones* of the Elder Philostratus. But as we now know, this text was itself an "artfully composed representation of viewing" rather than a pattern for describing art works, while *ekphrasis* aimed less at describing an object than at rivaling painting "using its own resources."[36] Byzantine *ekphraseis* are not straightforward descriptions. Whether of secular or religious objects, they demonstrate both the enormous influence on Byzantine writing of rhetoric and the Second

Sophistic and the intimate relation in Byzantium between rhetoric and visual art. Rather than taking them as direct responses to the art works in question (as has often been done), as indications of a theory of viewing, or as expressive of the responses of a contemporary viewer, each example needs to be subjected to its own detailed literary critique. Only then can it can be used (if at all) to interpret the artwork in question. Do art and text work in parallel, then, or should we not rather say that they are intertwined?

As in other matters, too, interpreting visual art in Byzantium is made more difficult by its complex and ongoing relation with earlier historical periods. As I argued in chapter 1, appreciation of Byzantine literature has been impeded for decades by the emphasis placed by traditional scholarship on *mimesis*, translated as "imitation." According to this view, which is only now coming under serious scrutiny, Byzantine literature and Byzantine culture more generally were inherently derivative and unoriginal. Byzantium also suffers in the judgments made of its visual art, even if not in the same way. Like other Byzantine writers, the authors of *ekphraseis* inherited rhetorical strategies and assumptions from the writers of the Second Sophistic who remained their literary models. Unlike ourselves, they evidently felt that there was no awkwardness in applying the same tropes and terminology to what seems now to be the very different visual art of Byzantium.

At a deeper level, interpreting the art of Byzantium suffers from the modern confusion of periodization between "Byzantium" and late antiquity, a period in whose visual art many of the same issues

Figure 8. Not all Byzantine art was sacred: these undignified male dancers are carved on the lid of a bone casket. ▪ Photo © The Walters Art Museum, Baltimore

arise (figure 8). Byzantium is not an autonomous subject, in other words. On the one hand, late antiquity (otherwise referred to as "early Byzantium") has been seen as an "age of spirituality," in which visual art not only became progressively more religious, but more religious in a specific way. On the other, features and issues that are found in the art of Byzantium have been shown to have roots not merely in late antique but also in Roman art.[37] As with the search for a "Byzantine" identity, discussed in chapter 2, Byzantium cannot be taken in isolation either from its roots in the Roman imperial period or from late antiquity.

Scholars dealing with Byzantine literature are visibly struggling, not only with the dominant concept of imitation, much discussed in other fields of literary theory, but also with the undeniable habit of Byzantine authors to draw explicitly on classical models, to incorporate direct quotations, and to use archaizing vocabulary.[38] All this also applies to Byzantine writers on visual art, which itself engaged with its past on many different levels. But finding citations and parallels is one thing; interpreting their use is quite another. Like the abundant recent scholarship on the Second Sophistic, many recent contributions about Roman art are also vital for the understanding of Byzantine literature and art.

Seen in this light, Byzantine art loses some of its exceptionalism. Its interpretation also falls within an overall move among art historians away from style and iconography toward issues of representation, semiotics, and the responses of "the viewer." But the question has been further complicated by the fact that in earlier historiography the period we now call late antiquity was inexorably associated with a hermeneutics of decadence and decline. How then could Byzantine art be viewed except as further evidence of inferiority? These ideas were the context against which the aesthetes and travelers discussed earlier were so fascinated by their discovery of Byzantine art in the early twentieth century: the exotic appeal that it exercised on them involved what for them was a daring rejection of conventional classicism. Yet it was an art historian, Alois Riegl, who developed a groundbreaking rejection of "decline," precisely in relation to the early Byzantine or "late antique" period, and thereby initiated the current more positive view of late antiquity.[39] How to link the interpretation of the art of late antiquity with that of the later centuries of Byzantium presents a challenge. In relation to visual art at least, to claim that "Byzantium" began only in the seventh century or thereabouts (chapter 1) risks cutting off some of the most important and best-known examples of Byzantine art: it clearly does not work.

Certainly the connection of Byzantine art with the intense arguments that went on about Orthodoxy and authority throughout the Byzantine period (themselves constituting a debate about truth and the status of communication) produced a particularly dense amount of theorizing and textual commentary, bequeathing to modern interpreters a range of intriguing problems. It was one of the legacies of the eighth-century and ninth-century theoretical debates about images that visual art was for Byzantines not only a central topic within the discourse of religious orthodoxy, but can itself actually be said to have constituted Orthodoxy. Art, especially in the form of icons, became a form of religious exegesis. It therefore needed to be interpreted itself, and the level of anxiety about true representation led to the development of rules, or at least conventions, for artists, even if they were never as clear-cut, or as strictly observed, as used to be believed. Recognition of the agendas lying behind many individual works designed to expound and claim their various versions of orthodox doctrine, and their capacity to enunciate complex theological themes in visual terms, has been part of the move among Byzantine art historians toward a highly contextual exposition and away from the stylistic analysis . To be a Byzantine art historian at this juncture requires a highly sophisticated theological awareness combined with the deployment of complex and often obscure theological texts. And since so much

Byzantine writing of this kind remains imperfectly edited or is even unpublished, this means that they must be philologists, theologians, and liturgists, too.

I have been concerned here with images and the intellectual theory of representation. But icons also communicated in other ways. There is no doubt about their spiritual effects on viewers, and they could also constitute an important part within a sacred space that involved liturgical performance, incense and perfume, sound, touch, and visual perception. More than that, icons could themselves be "performative," as in the case of the great icons of late Byzantium and their associated rituals—some acquired an animated and miraculous life of their own.[40] This was also recognized in the dressing of icons with veils and silk, and their encasement in covers made of precious metals. It was a development licensed by the theological and intellectual debates of the eighth, and especially the ninth, century. At the same time, it needs to be recognized that many icons and other examples of visual art in Byzantium were inevitably quite routine or clichéd: not every icon had "a simple aesthetic beauty,"[41] not every work can be a masterpiece, and not every work reached the level of complexity that I have suggested. But it remains true that visual art in Byzantium requires exegesis as well as aesthetic appreciation,[42] and that in many cases the object itself constitutes an exegetical reading of its subject.

So far this chapter has dealt mainly with religious art in Byzantium, and especially with visual art. In contrast with the approach

I have just described, some art historians prefer to cast their subject in terms of a discussion of "material culture." This is partly due to unease with theological agendas and with the overrepresentation of Orthodox approaches in the secondary literature on Byzantium. Another motive is the desire to find an alternative to aesthetic judgments; yet another stems from the aim of locating these artifacts in the realm of production, exchange, and economics. Crafts, artisanal production, and production techniques also belong to the subject matter of Byzantine art history, as do the roles of patrons, donors, and patronage. Given the discursive turn in art history, as well as the volume of Byzantine theoretical writing about images, it is not surprising if the already vast literature on icons has proliferated (and been given priority in this chapter). But the great increase in archaeological investigation and the vast amount of data now available for the eastern empire, especially in the earlier period, also invite more technical, as well as more quantitative, approaches to material culture.

The availability of archaeological data also invites an interdisciplinary methodology, especially drawing on anthropological literature. Here the new interdisciplinary field of "material culture studies" may well have some lessons for Byzantinists.[43] Alfred Gell's *Art and Agency*, published in 1998 (chapter 2),[44] proposed an arresting interpretation of material objects in given cultures, including artworks, as themselves constituting agents in social life; it would be interesting to see this applied to the material culture of Byzantium.

Art historians are not the only ones who have problems in interpreting Byzantium. The discipline of art history has played an important and central role in the development of Byzantine studies, and publications in this field account for a large proportion of the whole. But Byzantine art history cannot be left to its own specialists. It cannot stand alone.

CHAPTER 5

The Very Model of Orthodoxy?

Was Byzantium an "Orthodox society"?

Most scholars from countries with Orthodox churches of their own (Greece, Russia, Bulgaria, Serbia, Macedonia, to name only the most obvious) take this for granted. So indeed do most of the rest of us. Almost everyone is influenced by what we think we know: that there was a split between the eastern and western churches, in which Byzantium represented "eastern Orthodoxy" in opposition to the west, and especially to the papacy. For most, the Crusades provide irrefutable evidence of the depth of the split. On the other hand—and this is less well known—there was also a divide between Constantinople and places farther east, with the development of the "Jacobite" or Syrian Orthodox church; the "Church of the East" (commonly but incorrectly known as Nestorian), which in the seventh century had already penetrated as far east as China; and the rise of Coptic Christianity in Egypt. All these also thought of themselves as Orthodox. So did the Armenians, who were nevertheless the subject over many centuries of Byzantine efforts to square this circle.

Meanwhile Arnold Toynbee's concept of an "Orthodox civilization," contrasted with that of the west, reappears in current writing, even if Francis Fukuyama's premature declaration of western superiority has now been tarnished.[1] As we have seen (chapter 2), the gentler and more local idea of an "Orthodox commonwealth" enshrined by Dimitri Obolensky also still has purchase, not least in Orthodox countries, as do the concepts of an Orthodox world and an Orthodox worldview.[2] So here is another problematic subject in relation to Byzantium—more problematic than most interpreters assume.

This chapter does not attempt to describe the full range of the Byzantine religious framework, and still less Byzantine religious experience or the *habitus* of religious life.[3] Many accounts, especially when written from the Orthodox point of view, emphasize the sense of direct spiritual access to God to be found in the writings of such authors as Ps. Dionysius the Areopagite, Maximus Confessor, or Symeon the New Theologian, and this is indeed a prominent feature of religiosity in Byzantium. The weekly and annual round of the liturgy and feast days, with their homilies, prescribed readings from the Gospels and the lives of the saints, and the visual impact of icons and religious art, worked on the consciousness of ordinary people and elites alike. A powerful strand in Greek patristic thought maintained that the nature of God could be understood only through negatives and could not be encompassed in the language of rational argument. Yet Orthodoxy was also perceived as a system accessible to reason (theology), as we saw manifested in the preceding chapter in the arguments over religious images. A massive effort was indeed made throughout the

Byzantine period to articulate the nature of God—in particular, the exact relation between the three persons of the Trinity. The series of ecclesiastical councils from the Council of Nicaea in AD 325 to the Council of Chalcedon in AD 451 were recognized in Constantinople as authoritative, even though the Council of Ephesus in AD 431 and that of Chalcedon in 451 led to the formation of separatist eastern churches. But the struggle to formulate and defend Orthodox belief continued to the very end of Byzantium.

Byzantine emperors and ecclesiastics alike tried to impose authority at all levels, with what success in relation to the general population it is hard to tell. Byzantine official art promoted the idea of hierarchy, with the emperor at the peak on earth and reflecting the hierarchy of the divine,[4] and emperor, patriarch,[5] higher clergy, and monastic leaders alike all engaged in a performance of Orthodoxy (see later). Yet despite the growth of church legislation (canon law), real authority remained dispersed and challenged; it depended on a shifting mix of negotiation, manipulation, and personal influence within the secular and ecclesiastical network. The western idea of papal primacy remained a stumbling block for Byzantines over many centuries, but in resisting it they were forced onto the defensive and had to rely on tradition rather than any clear equivalent of their own. Religious authority in Byzantium remained contested and open to challenge, as did the imperial throne, and the Byzantines themselves did not speak with one voice. It is hard to speak of a single "church" in such circumstances.

This chapter will be concerned with the nature of these contests, and with the extraordinary lengths to which contemporaries went to defend and negotiate their own positions. It departs from traditionalist ideas of heresies as external threats to an essentialist Orthodoxy and sees the Orthodox system itself as the product of struggles over definition that continued over many centuries.[6]

Orthodoxy in Byzantium grew directly out of developments in early Christianity and the patristic period. The first question, therefore, is when—or if—the search for orthodoxy that had been apparent in early Christianity and that continued throughout the Roman empire and late antiquity was transformed into "Orthodoxy"—that is, a distinct system. A favorite date (in fact rather late, since others prefer ca. 600 or sometime in the seventh or eighth centuries) is the mid-ninth century, with the formal ending of iconoclast policies and what the Byzantines themselves called "the triumph of Orthodoxy" in 843.[7] We might seem to have a watershed in the contemporary formulation of the so-called *Synodikon* of Orthodoxy, to which I have already referred, a highly symbolic document setting out what was to count as Orthodox, and (even more importantly) condemning what was not.[8] But in fact such a document had many precedents, and, as I have argued, we now know more clearly just how much the "event" of the ending of iconoclasm was in reality a matter of intense manipulation (figure 9). The document was subsequently read out in a liturgical context, and indeed is still read today, but it was not sacrosanct, and as we have seen in the case of John Italus (chapter 2), it received

Figure 9. This icon from the British Museum, painted about 1400, is known as *The Triumph of Orthodoxy* because it depicts in several scenes and in symbolic fashion the ending of iconoclasm in 843. Here the young emperor Michael III and his mother the empress Theodora stand next to the famous icon of the Theotokos Hodegetria, which no longer survives. The patriarch Methodius stands to the right of the icon. ▪ Image © The Trustees of the British Museum

later additions as new "heretics" were identified and formally condemned.[9]

The process that led to these additions being made during the eleventh century was very far from straightforward, and the centuries before the *Synodikon* had also seen a procession of such formal statements, from the synodical letters of bishops like of Sophronius of Jerusalem in the seventh century to the resolutions and documents of the great councils (Nicaea, 325; Constantinople I, 380; Ephesus, 431; Chalcedon, 451; Constantinople II, 553; the Lateran Synod, 649; the Sixth Council, 680–81; the iconoclast council of Hieria, 754; II Nicaea, 787; and the further iconoclast council of 815, to name only the most central). The fact that the second council of Nicaea in 787 was regarded in the east as the last of the seven ecumenical councils, and depicted as such in visual art, did not mean that there were no further divisions, any more than the increase in monastic foundations and now-unhindered production of religious images and figural schemes of church decoration from the ninth century onward meant that all was now settled. Neither the "draining of the secular," thought to characterize the onset of the middle ages,[10] nor the undoubted fascination that many now have for the idea of eastern spirituality should blind us to something that was in practice much more complex.

In an important way, this issue is about the disagreements about essentialism and anti-essentialism discussed in chapter 3. But other difficulties also lie in the way of approaches to Byzantine Orthodoxy. It has also been a feature of histories of Byzantium, for instance, that the history of Orthodoxy has been seen as belonging to its own sphere of "ecclesiastical" or "church" history and presented in terms of emperors and patriarchs, or more widely, emperors, bishops, and monks. Little attempt has yet been made to subject Byzantine Orthodoxy to the kind of analysis by specialists in the study of religion that is standard for other periods. We know a great deal about religious phenomena and practices, theological and other kinds of religious literature, religious structures and spirituality, but the theoretical underpinning that would allow the understanding that the subject calls for is so far conspicuous by its absence. It would mark a considerable advance if the same energies that we saw in chapter 1 being applied to Byzantine literature were also extended to the field of religion.

This situation is compounded by questions about the status of Byzantine philosophy and its relation to theology. It has often been assumed that the former had no autonomous existence, all Byzantine thinking being automatically a matter of theology. However, this deep-seated idea is currently receiving a serious challenge as philosophers look again at Byzantine philosophy and make the case for its autonomy as against theology[11]—difficult though this is when so many key works remain to be edited. The search for dissent in Byzantium, whether articulated or hidden, is a further reaction to the standard view (chapter 2).[12] But behind these current debates lies a deeper question about the nature of Orthodoxy: was it so hegemonic and dominant a system that any intellectual independence from it was necessarily forced to find expression in dissimulation, or should we see Byzantine Orthodoxy less as a system than a mixture of tenets and practices that were themselves liable to challenge and that needed strenuous and repeated efforts to promote and enforce—in fact, a continual performance, constantly revised and constantly renewed? It is striking to observe in relation to the present uncertainties about Byzantine philosophy and its relation to Orthodoxy that the discussion tends to focus on a limited number of intellectuals from the ninth to the twelfth centuries, whose positions are from a modern point of view extremely hard to assess. Their ambiguity reflects the ambiguities of the period in religious and intellectual authority and in the Byzantine educational system, with its uncertain line between philosophy and rhetoric and surprising (to us) lack of specifically theological training. Seen in this light it becomes easier to understand how individuals combined ecclesiastical and lay positions in their own careers, as well as what pressures they faced in their lives and writing.[13] But we should be cautious about positing a hidden strand of rationalising opposition.

Last, because so many of those who write about Byzantine Orthodoxy do so from an Orthodox position themselves (and because the very frequency of doctrinal division and debate in Byzantium means that there is such a mass of surviving textual material), there has been a strong focus on doctrine and theology, and far less on orthopraxy, *habitus* or "lived Orthodoxy." And as I have already mentioned, even less has so far been written about Byzantium from the point of view of the sociology or anthropology of religion.[14] I cannot pretend that this chapter provides such an analysis, but at least it provides a warning against taking the evidence at face value; definitions of "religion," and of "orthodoxy" in relation to Byzantium have to be the starting point.

The centrality of Orthodoxy in Byzantium cannot be disputed. Yet the lack of a central authority or *magisterium* exposed it to constant challenge. Many emperors spent time and strenuous efforts to settle disputes or sometimes to impose doctrines, and as emperors they had important religious prerogatives; but the emperor was not head of the church and could not simply impose his will. The patriarchs of Constantinople might oppose the emperor, but might also be deposed by him.[15] All sides participated in a competitive appeal to the authority of the Greek Fathers. If Byzantine high-level culture as a whole was "logocentric,"[16] this was certainly true of its conception of Orthodoxy. Such an emphasis, combined with the perceived need to cite and interpret patristic authorities for every doctrinal statement, might seem to lead to inescapable deadlock, had it not been for the convenient Byzantine principle of "economy" or flexibility, which could be invoked to resolve an otherwise insoluble situation.[17]

The decentralization of religious authority in Byzantium was a distinct disadvantage when it came to debates with the Latins. Another disadvantage in the discussions was the fact that there was no equivalent to the new scholastic training that developed in the west. Indeed, in Byzantine higher education (a conglomerate of teachers, posts, and private "schools") the dividing line between philosophy and rhetoric was blurred,[18] like that between theology and philosophy, and theological teaching as such was not included. Especially in later Byzantium, numerous individuals moved without undue difficulty between "chairs," court posts, and ecclesiastical appointments, and it was not uncommon for the holders of teaching posts to leave and enter monastic orders. The habit of relying in theological argument on authoritative citations from the Greek Fathers had been built up very early, and was taken for granted. "Florilegia" (selected passages) of citations were available to aid specific arguments; this was more than a mere matter of copying earlier material, in that individual writers also compiled their own lists and sought ways of reconciling any apparently contradictory statements by the Fathers.

A deep ambivalence also existed about the very techniques of argument. Aristotle's logical works were much used and studied, and syllogistic reasoning frequently adopted, but at the same time "syllogizing" and "Aristotelianism" were condemned as unsuitable to theological issues.[19] It could be enough to describe a rival (especially of course a Latin), as arguing "syllogistically," with the implication that Greek argument was "simple," pure, and authentic. Eustratius of Nicaea in the twelfth century (see later) was one who was brought down by this kind of accusation.

Most emperors liked to see themselves as guardians of religious correctness. They were well aware of the practical dangers of division, and often went to great lengths to try to heal it. This was by no means always successful, as many found when they tried it.

Sometimes their own policies created division—especially over the issue of union with the Latins—as did their choice of patriarch. Many emperors faced vehement opposition from church leaders over their own actions or their doctrinal positions.

Sometimes the evidence allows us to see emperors in action, to get a taste of the problems they faced and how they tried to deal with them. One such example concerns the emperor Alexius I Comnenus (1081–1118), and it will be worth looking at it at some length as a test case.

Faced with acute military needs when he became emperor, Alexius ordered precious materials from churches to be melted down for the imperial treasure, to an immediate outcry. The leader of the opposition was Leo, the well-connected metropolitan of Chalcedon; such was the uproar that the emperor had to step back, though he later resorted again to similar measures. Meanwhile Leo kept up his opposition and was eventually forced into exile. Writing about this episode so early in her father's reign, Alexius's daughter, the historian Anna Comnena, admits that Leo's views received considerable support,[20] and he continued to circulate them by letter. His letter to the bishop of Adrianople became public and caused more trouble. As Anna makes very clear, Alexius could not afford this opposition to continue, and his brother Isaac's justificatory compilation of patristic and conciliar citations was not enough to end the matter. Eustratius, metropolitan of Nicaea, one of the best theological debaters of his day, as well as a commentator on Aristotle, produced a defense of the emperor's actions in the form of a dialogue.

Whereas Leo's position was that the material from which icons were made was itself also the carrier of the divine and therefore must be immune from any destruction, Eustratius argued in favor of the view conventional since the ninth century that only the image itself related to the divine, not the material from which it was made.[21] Finally the emperor chose to assert himself: late in 1094 Alexius summoned and presided over a synod held at Blachernae, as a result of which Leo formally recanted. With this mixture of strong-arm tactics and politics it might seem as though the affair was settled.

The synod's proceedings are also worth a closer look.[22] The emperor began from the offending letter written by Leo to Nicholas of Adrianople, and called together members of the senate, bishops, and monks in an assembly in the recently rebuilt great triclinium of the imperial palace of Blachernae. The names of those present are listed in the surviving document, and the emperor's brother Isaac and the patriarchs of Constantinople and Jerusalem sat with Alexius as judges.[23] The emperor himself opened the meeting, proposed prayers, and summoned Leo; he then ordered Leo and his correspondent to be reconciled, and they embraced "like brothers." Extracts were then read out from the acts of the second Council of Nicaea in 787, which had restored icons, and all present affirmed their acceptance. Alexius then announced the position that he said had been held to be Orthodox since the time of Theodore the Studite in the ninth century: the material of images, as opposed to the actual representation of Christ, should not be accorded worship. Anyone who disagreed was to be anathematized—that is, formally condemned.[24] In the eighth century even the iconoclastic council of Hieria had forbidden the laying on of hands on the holy vessels, including by emperors,[25] but Alexius claimed that his interpretation had been confirmed by the apostles, the prophets, the Fathers, Christ Himself, and the synods. More questions followed, and when Leo was asked whether he accepted the teachings of Theodore the Studite he agreed, thus repudiating his letter. No one else spoke out; all agreed "from first to last."

The written proceedings constitute an official document, and as such naturally present the result of the meeting in terms favorable to the emperor. In this case Alexius got his way, and it may well seem as if what the emperor ordained was invariably accepted. This was far from the case. It is very clear that Leo's recantation (made in public, as had also been required since late antiquity of anyone who abjured Manichaeanism, Judaism, or Islam, or other heretical beliefs) was achieved only at the cost of considerable effort, including the marshaling by experts of the necessary arguments by which he could be refuted. This was the function of Eustratius's dialogue and its accompanying "Demonstration" [*Apodeixis*] in the form of syllogistic reasoning.[26] The dialogue was the equivalent of a modern dossier brought to support an unpopular government initiative.

The emperor was discomfited when Eustratius's use of Aristotelian syllogisms brought him under suspicion as well, and Alexius was compelled to accede to his deposition (1117). This process too can be followed in surviving documents, which are even more instructive for the interplay between emperor, patriarch, and senior churchmen, and give us a precious insight into the realities of the time.[27] Eustratius's use of Aristotelian dialectic was made a point of contention, and after a long period as Alexius's approved theologian, he was deemed by his enemies to have overreached himself in the course of debates with the Armenians. Alexius did his best to protect him. He and the patriarch lobbied members of the synod before it met to decide the case on 11 April 1117. A compromise was reached: emperor and patriarch presided together, and Eustratius duly recanted his statements and asked for forgiveness. But a second session, at which Alexius was not present, required a statement of faith from Eustratius. The patriarch, sympathetic to the emperor's wishes, argued with references to the need for "economy," that Eustratius should receive the lightest possible punishment—namely, temporary suspension. But only eight out of twenty-two synod members agreed, even then admitting that they had been previously lobbied to do so, while nine voted for a severer penalty. The archbishop of Leontopolis went further and called for Eustratius's errors to be formally added to the *Synodikon of Orthodoxy.* The emperor was present at the final meeting after a further adjournment, and was voted down. The *Synodikon* was amended, Eustratius anathematized, and his offending works burned.[28] Alexius's daughter Anna Comnena passes over her father's defeat in total silence. Modern opinions may emphasize Alexius I's efforts during his reign to control religious opinion,[29] but here is a clear case of an emperor being ousted.

Emperors could also be the targets of ecclesiastical condemnation themselves, like Heraclius (610–41), who had married his niece, Martina; Leo VI (866–912), who married four times; or Michael VIII Palaeologus (1259–82), excommunicated by the patriarch Arsenius for his blinding and relegation of the young heir John IV, and later opposed by many for his unionist policy enunciated in the Union of Lyons (1274). Emperors often met such opposition by deposing and replacing the patriarch in question; but this was a risky response, apt to create yet more division. Certainly emperors could use the resources of the state against religious opponents, and sometimes they resorted to imprisonment as well as exile. The example had been set many centuries before by Constantine, who also professed himself ready to use force against the recalcitrant Donatists in North Africa. But Constantine had the fiery indignation of someone new to church affairs; for his later successors intervening in such matters was a more complex business. When in the last year of his reign Manuel I Comnenus (1143–80) wanted to encourage Muslim conversion to Christianity by softening the required abjuration formula, the ecclesiastical synod led by the patriarch rejected his arguments on two separate occasions; a compromise was eventually reached but not without forceful expostulations from Eustathius, the well-known archbishop of Thessalonike.[30]

Already in late antiquity there had been a vast technologizing of theological argument, through collections of citations, sets of questions and answers, treatises, commentaries, exegetical works, and theological discussions,[31] and this developed even further in Byzantium. When divisions arose it was assumed that they could be settled only by resorting to an armory of proof texts and learned argument; indeed, the heresiological compilations of Euthymius Zigabenus and Andronicus Camaterus in the eleventh and twelfth centuries are known respectively as the *Dogmatic Panoply* and the *Sacred Arsenal* ("dogmatic armor" and "sacred weapons"). Codifications and compilations provided the indispensable equipment for theological controversy, and in the eighth century, John of Damascus had composed his *Fount of Knowledge* on just such principles. As we have it, it consists of three parts: first, the *Dialectics*; second, *On Heresies*, a compilation listing one hundred heresies, an expansion of earlier works of similar type;[32] and third, *On the Orthodox Faith*, a comprehensive guide to orthodox doctrine, also in a hundred chapters.

Historians find this material hard to deal with. Reviewing the very large theological output of the twelfth century, Paul Magdalino comments: "The arguments presented by all this literature are . . . derivative in the extreme, and this despite the disingenuousness of their authors' claim to eschew syllogistic method and demonstrative proof. Theology, it seems, was not allowed to share in the cultural expression of the age."[33] He gives the example of the *Dogmatic Panoply* of Zigabenus, commissioned by Alexius I and mentioned earlier, which "both symbolized and heralded a growing mood of entrenchment against doctrinal outsiders"—Jews, Muslims, dualists, Monophysites, Armenians, and finally Latins.[34] In fact the *Dogmatic Panoply* represented little that was new; it followed a pattern that had been set many centuries before, when Christian doctrine was finding its first technical expression.[35] In his critique of twelfth-century theological writing Magdalino also includes the several theological works written in the form of dialogues, some of them literary productions, others claiming to be either transcripts, or edited or expanded records of real encounters. Yet a closer look shows that they vary considerably in tone and content. While the chronological spread of such dialogues is uneven, they were composed at all periods of Byzantine history. They cannot be written off as pointless or quaintly archaizing productions.

The same discussion prompts reflections about religious toleration or intolerance in Byzantium (chapter 2).[36] Byzantium produced a harsh rhetoric of condemnation at all levels of society, but it was a premodern society and, like the Roman empire before it, lacked the apparatus of enforcement that would have been necessary to carry it all through (figure 10).[37] Bishops could be deposed and exiled, and often were, but this was another inheritance from the early Christian centuries; despite some show trials and much rhetoric about heresy late Byzantium did not (and was in no position to) develop anything like an Inquisition.

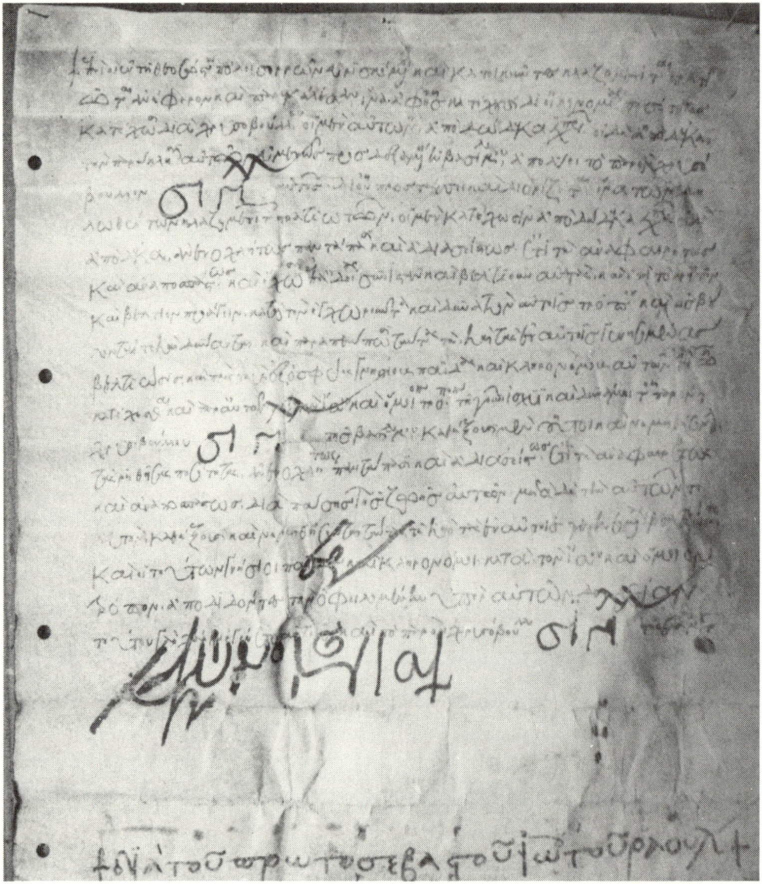

Figure 10. A chrysobull—that is, a document with the emperor's gold seal (usually missing now) and his signature in red. This one was issued in 1342 by the emperor John V Palaeologus for the soldiers of Klazomenai, not far from modern Izmir. ▪ Image courtesy the Bayerische Akademie der Wissenschaften, München

Monks and monasteries constituted a major element in Byzantine society, but unlike the west Byzantium had no powerful monastic orders, and monks and holy men were as likely to be a decentralizing and centrifugal force as an integrative one. In early Byzantium monks often played a role in urban unrest, and the iconophile monks of the Studios monastery in Constantinople were closely involved in the contests over icons; their abbot, Theodore, was imprisoned. Circumstances differed at different periods, but individual holy men (usually monastics) could be divisive elements, as well as the objects of profound respect for emperors and elite as well as ordinary people.[38] Monasteries played many roles over and above that of being repositories of Byzantine spirituality: they were also useful for instance as places of exile, as safe retreats from awkward situations, as sources of income and recipients of personal patronage, and as aristocratic retirement homes, all in the complex interplay of interest and rivalry that characterized Byzantine religious society.

Historians no longer believe that the so-called Great Schism of 1054 put an end to contacts between the eastern and western churches. Yet for a period of five centuries thereafter Byzantium was engaged in a complex, emotional, and difficult tangle centering on the differences of doctrine and practice between east and west. This was compounded from the late eleventh century onward by the manifold and complex impact of the Crusades on Byzantium, the changing policies of the papacy, developments within Latin theology and the advent of scholasticism, and not least the pressing need of the east for western assistance against threats from the Turks. Some emperors and some churchmen were prepared to accept papal primacy and the addition of the word *filioque* to the Creed; many others were passionately opposed. This division continued even after the great unionist council of Ferrara/Florence in 1438–39 and up to the last days of Byzantine Constantinople. It has been easy for historians to regard the doctrinal intransigence displayed by many in late Byzantium as a hopeless rearguard action, and to leave the theological issues to specialists.[39] This is a mistake. In the fourteenth century bitter internal division raged over the teachings of Gregory Palamas, and was only settled after several councils had been held; the last, in 1351, anathematized, deposed, and imprisoned Palamas's opponents, and had their writings burned (figure 11). The real challenge for historians is to do justice to the vast effort and passion that went into these issues, including the outpouring of writing and debate that was dedicated to them. Such an endeavor could start by editing, commenting on, and translating the many works still not so studied (which some scholars are indeed doing), but it also cries out for the kind of analytic historiographical approach that has been applied to similar materials in earlier periods.

It still remains to investigate the concept of an "Orthodox culture."[40] What might such a concept mean, and can it be accepted? In Magdalino's formulation, it was a development of the seventh and eighth centuries, and was cemented by the official "ending" of iconoclasm in 843.[41] This is to cut Byzantium off from its roots and

Figure 11. The emperor John VI Cantacuzenus (1347–54) surrounded by bishops at the council of 1351 in the Blachernae church in Constantinople. This council finally affirmed the teachings of Gregory Palamas and anathematized his opponents. ▪ Ms Gr 1242 fol.5v John VI (ca.1292–1383) Cantacuzene, President of the Council of Constantinople (vellum), 1351, Byzantine (14th century) / Bibliotheque Nationale, Paris, France / Flammarion / Giraudon / The Bridgeman Art Library

to ignore the difficult forging of the concept of "Orthodoxy" in late antiquity and indeed in the early Christian period; it also obscures the ways in which the emphasis laid on orthodoxy in later Byzantium was a continuation of those processes.[42] Magdalino then says he will consider the concept of an orthodox culture by looking at the importance that the Byzantines attached to orthodoxy or to being Orthodox; again, this was not new—it had been the case for centuries—nor does it address the problem of what is meant by a "culture."[43] It is indeed easy to find in the texts assertions of adherence to the idea of correct doctrine, combined with the idea of divine favor for those who got it right; but one can look back even before the emperor Constantine in the fourth century, for very similar expressions. They did not prevent disagreement; nor were these sentiments necessarily shared by all. And while certain kinds of visual art were given free reign after 843 (chapter 4), the iconophiles who saw themselves as winning the day were engaged less in a "systematic attempt to create an Orthodox Christian doctrine for a new Chosen People"[44] than (as much recent scholarship has made very clear) in an invention of tradition and a rewriting of recent history. It is only now that the full extent of such rewriting by the victorious iconophiles has begun to be fully recognized. But if there was now a "general climate of piety," in Magdalino's words, exemplified in florilegia, pastoral didacticism, and apocalyptic, how was this different from earlier periods when the same kinds of writing flourished equally strongly? It is in any case almost impossible to grasp what ordinary people actually believed in a society for which we have little direct access. Still less should we envisage a kind of Orthodox command culture, though Magdalino goes on to argue that this late "creation of an Orthodox culture" was the result of deliberate planning, or at least a high degree of "programming"[45]

The question needs to be put differently. Once the the notion of Christian orthodoxy developed, by the second century AD at the latest, the term was claimed by all interested parties, with momentous, and many would say damaging, results for the future history of Christianity, both eastern and western. The symbolic date of 843 was much vaunted by the successful iconophiles and their successors, but while it was taken to signify the end of a difficult period, the significance attached to it in later periods gives the impression that something new had happened and obscures the ways in which Byzantine religious culture had been already been shaped before the eighth and ninth centuries.

To return to the notion of an "Orthodox culture" in Byzantium: if such a thing existed at all, and especially given the importance attached to the idea of flexibility ("economy"), it may be that it could best be understood by looking for resistance and disagreement. If Byzantium can hardly be described without anachronism as a tolerant society, the totalitarian Byzantium of some scholars is equally anachronistic.[46] We can readily agree that in Byzantium, as elsewhere in the medieval world, religion provided both the discursive framework and the norms of ordinary life. In that sense the concept of an Orthodox culture does not tell us much. But appealing to it in a stronger sense, not merely of an overarching concept but of something universally accepted and unquestioned, obscures the actual tensions and fissures that existed at different times as much in Byzantium as in any other society. I have tried here to lay emphasis on some of these, but the challenge remains: to do justice to Byzantine religious culture in all its real complexity.

I have argued in this chapter that Orthodoxy in Byzantium was always vaunted but also always contested. The constant performance of Orthodoxy took many forms: they included imperial ceremonial, liturgical repetition and display, visual representation, public debates, formal anathemas and recantations, declarations of deposition, and the public reading of documents.[47] Yet the actual evidence for the various councils that supported or condemned religious images shows clearly that in Byzantium as elsewhere ecclesiastics changed sides, negotiated their positions, and adapted their views. The example of the synods held in the reign of Alexius I also demonstrates both the degree of preparation that was necessary and the uncertainty of the outcomes. Nor indeed were doctrine and belief all that mattered. Orthopraxy was also important, and the liturgy and the material apparatus of worship induced a shared *habitus* that was reinforced by the moral regulations enshrined in canon law and preached in countless homilies. Ordinary habits such as visiting particular shrines and venerating particular saints also mattered. In many areas under Byzantine rule a practical multiculturalism prevailed, especially where populations had moved or political control fluctuated, and this too is part of the story of Byzantine religion.

Yet the very word "orthodoxy" means correct belief, and the articulation of correct doctrine remained a central issue throughout Byzantine history. Rules and prescriptions characterized Byzantine Orthodoxy. Our challenge is to take this seriously and ask what it meant. I have called already in this chapter for the application to Byzantium of the kind of approaches brought to the study of religion in early Christianity, the Roman empire, and late antiquity. A further advance that would transform the understanding of Byzantine Orthodoxy in its social and political context would be the application to Byzantine texts of the rhetorical and discourse analysis that has been applied in recent years for instance to the legal texts of the Roman empire and especially of late antiquity, which has led to a completely different conception of how law actually worked (and especially of its limitations).[48] As I pointed out in chapter 1, Byzantine literary texts are currently the subject of lively reexamination, and the same needs to happen for religious and theological writing. Meanwhile, as long as religious language and theological rhetoric in Byzantine texts remain so understudied and undertheorized, they will continue to be accepted at face value, or conversely, ignored as irrelevant. Byzantium will remain what it has always been—an exotic and unchanging other.

Epilogue

> A new and in many ways significantly revised version of Byzantine history is obviously in the making.
>
> —Johann P. Arnason[1]

After discussing the ways in which the subject has moved on from the immensely influential synthesis of Ostrogorsky, the author of the preceding words also writes: "No similarly authoritative overall interpretation has emerged from recent debates."[2] Instead, in addition to many excellent contributions on specific subjects, we have the plethora of guides, companions, handbooks, and edited volumes already noted. Arnason lists the prejudices about Byzantium that he believes have been overcome: belief in "caesaropapism," imperial control of the church; Byzantine continuity from the Roman empire, but in inferior form; lack of dynamism and originality; and the failure to see Byzantium in its wider contexts or its "active role in the networks and processes that linked it to western Christendom and Islam."[3]

Nevertheless, this book has been concerned with the difficulties of interpretation that still seem to stand in the way of understanding Byzantium. Many elements important to Byzantine history are not considered here—they include not only warfare and military matters, law, administration, and economy but also the huge field of hagiography and other aspects relating to social history. Byzantium certainly needs a fresh look in relation to both the west and Islam. My main preoccupation here has been with the historiography of the subject, and the ways in which it has been (and still is) seen, both in the secondary literature and more widely. I am very aware that these essays focus on articulate elite culture in Byzantium rather than on its wider social history (and that even so there is little discussion of the imperial center). Yet it remains true that at its higher levels Byzantium was a learned culture, the nature of which is still not fully understood or appreciated. It was also a highly competitive, and in premodern terms open, society, in which in most periods learning and especially rhetorical skill provided a pathway to advancement.

However much one wishes to avoid the dangers of seeming to argue for continuity, it is impossible to avoid the question of periodization in relation to Byzantium. As I have noted, several recent writers prefer to see "Byzantium" proper as beginning from ca. 600 or later, and there are good reasons why. Constantinople was formally inaugurated in AD 330, but there was not yet such an entity as "Byzantium," distinct from the eastern Roman empire, and it remains the case that the Byzantines thought of themselves as Romans (chapter 3). The shock and loss of territory consequent on the Arab invasions of the seventh century also necessitated a painful adjustment. Nevertheless, adopting a later periodization risks obscuring the fact that what we call Byzantium had a long earlier history; it was not a new state formed only in the medieval period.

In the last generation "late antiquity" has taken over from "the later Roman empire" in much of the secondary literature, even if the continuing number of publications discussing its scope and nature suggests that these questions are not yet settled. The "explosion" of late antiquity and now the turn to the east—that is, toward the eastern Mediterranean, the rise of Islam, and the early Islamic world—that is such a feature of current scholarship are both tendencies that threaten to squeeze out Byzantium. The danger, I fear, is that Byzantine scholarship may turn in on itself in response. In contrast, one of the arguments running through these essays has been that Byzantinists need to engage more directly with the relationship of Byzantine ideology, social practice, and artistic and intellectual features with what is now referred to as "late antiquity," especially given the huge amount of scholarship on the subject. One of the most difficult fields to incorporate into a wider understanding of Byzantium is the realm of theology and especially theological writing—just as it is also for late antique historians. Within the field of Byzantine Greek literary culture similar issues arise in relation to the role of rhetoric (where the far better understanding now reached by classicists and ancient historians of the many different aspects of the Second Sophistic needs also to be fully applied to Byzantium), and the relation of Byzantine literature to classical, over and beyond the traditional model of imitation.

Byzantium belongs to all of us, and it belongs to mainstream history.

This is why the field of Byzantine studies must be rescued from its continuing association with the competing claims of negativity and exoticism. Byzantine exceptionalism is an idea that holds us back. It is intimately connected with the idea of Byzantium as victim or subaltern. Recent publications have set an encouraging pattern. But now the subject needs to be opened up further, and Byzantium seen against more "normal" and wider perspectives.

NOTES

INTRODUCTION

1. Aaron Gurevich, "Why I Am Not a Byzantinist," *DOP* 46 (1992), 89–96, at 95–96.

2. Three major exhibitions have been held at the Metropolitan Museum of Art in New York: *Age of Spirituality: Late Antique and Early Christian Art* (1977); *The Glory of Byzantium: Art and Culture of the Middle Byzantine Era A.D. 843–1261* (1997); and *Byzantium: Faith and Power 1261–1557* (2004). They have been followed most recently by *Byzantium 330–1453* at the Royal Academy in London (2008–9) and by the Metropolitan Museum's exhibition on *Byzantium and Islam: Age of Transition, 7th–9th Century* (2012). I return to the theme of Byzantine art and its interpretation in chapter 4.

3. I am very grateful to my friend Professor János Bak of the Central European University, Budapest, for alerting me to this theme and to Professor Sergey A. Ivanov for letting me see a copy of his paper "The Second Rome as Seen by the Third: Russian Debates on 'The Byzantine Legacy,'" in *Byzantium Receptions*, ed. Dion Smythe and Przemyslaw Marciniak (Farnham, UK: Ashgate, 2014).

4. The trajectory of Byzantine studies in North America has been rather different, with many graduate students coming to the subject from a background in art history or general history.

5. The current enthusiasm shown among graduate students for learning Syriac, Coptic, and Arabic in places where such teaching is available is indeed remarkable, though it is usually connected with enthusiasm for late antiquity rather than Byzantium.

6. Fiona Haarer, "Writing Histories of Byzantium: The Historiography of Byzantine History," in *A Companion to Byzantium*, ed. Liz James (Chichester, UK: Wiley-Blackwell, 2010), 9–22, at 14.

7. It is invidious to single out individual examples, but one can point to

many individual and edited works by Cécile Morrisson, J.-P. Sodini, J. Lefort, and others, as well as introductions to Byzantium including *Le monde byzantin*, edited by Morrisson, Jean-Claude Cheynet, and Angeliki Laiou, 3 vols. (Paris: Presses Universitaires de France, 2004–11). The three-volume *Economic History of Byzantium*, edited by the late Angeliki E. Laiou and others (2002) was initiated and published at the Byzantine Research Center at Dumbarton Oaks in Washington, DC (part of Harvard University), where Laiou was the director, and which owns important collections of Byzantine coins and seals of officials. See also the very useful introduction by Angeliki Laiou and Cécile Morrisson, *The Byzantine Economy* (Cambridge, UK: Cambridge University Press, 2007).

8. The term derives from Andrea Giardina's well-known article, "Esplosione di tardoantico," *Studi storici* 40 (1999), 157–80, with English translation in *Late Antiquity on the Eve of Islam*, ed. Averil Cameron (Farnham, UK: Ashgate, 2011), 1–23.

9. Including Averil Cameron, *The Byzantines* (Oxford, UK: Blackwell, 2006).

Chapter 1. Absence

1. See chapter 5 for the iconoclastic controversy of the eighth and ninth centuries. The guidance is in the work known as the *De administrando imperio* ("On governing the empire"), one of a group of works composed and drawn up at the initiative of the emperor. They also include the *Book of Ceremonies*, a detailed codification of imperial ceremonial and protocol.

2. In all probability he was killed in the siege, but in the absence of a body, stories of his reappearance had a long life, and alleged descendants of Constantine XI were known as late as the twentieth century. The story is well told by Donald M. Nicol in *The Immortal Emperor: The Life and Legend of Constantine Palaiologos, Last Emperor of the Romans* (Cambridge, UK: Cambridge University Press, 1992).

3. The events of the final day, recorded in a variety of western, Greek, and Turkish sources, are movingly told by Steven Runciman, *The Fall of Constantinople, 1453* (Cambridge, UK: Cambridge University Press, 1965).

4. Take for instance Warren Treadgold, *A History of the Byzantine State and*

Society (Stanford, CA: Stanford University Press, 1997), part six, titled "The Failed Restoration" (that is, after 1204), in a book designed to be the modern replacement for G. Ostrogorsky's classic *History of the Byzantine State*, Eng. trans., 2nd ed. (Oxford, UK: Blackwell, 1968); H. J. Haussig, *Byzantine Civilization*, trans. J. M. Hussey (London: Thames and Hudson, 1971), part IV: "Byzantine Civilization in Decline." "Decline" is inscribed in the conception of Donald M. Nicol's *The Last Centuries of Byzantium, 1261–1453*, 2nd ed. (Cambridge, UK: Cambridge University Press, 1993), and indeed in the title of S. Ćurčič and Doula Mouriki, eds., *The Twilight of Byzantium: Aspects of Cultural and Religious History in the Late Byzantine Empire* (Princeton, NJ: Princeton University Press, 1991), while according to Stephen W. Reinert, in *The Oxford History of Byzantium*, ed. Cyril Mango (Oxford, UK: Oxford University Press, 2002), 248–83, at 248, "the once magnificent Byzantine empire seemingly devolves into little more than a caricature, a disordered and dysfunctional polity."

5. Cf. Edward Gibbon, *The History of the Decline and Fall of the Roman Empire*, ed. John B. Bury, 7 vols., 4th ed. (London: Methuen, 1896–1900), V.

6. Examples of this well-documented phenomenon include Romilly Jenkins, Donald Nicol, and Cyril Mango, all holders of the Koraes Chair of Modern Greek and Byzantine History, Language and Literature at King's College London; Mango's (brilliant) book, *Byzantium: Empire of New Rome* (London: Weidenfeld and Nicolson, 1980) gives the flavor of this approach.

7. Judith Herrin, *Byzantium: The Surprising Life of a Medieval Empire* (London: Allen Lane, 2007), explicitly and successfully eschews such negativity.

8. Byron's reactions are described by Peter Mackridge, "R. M. Dawkins and Byzantium," in *Through the Looking Glass. Byzantium through British Eyes*, ed. Robin Cormack and Elizabeth Jeffreys (Aldershot, UK: Ashgate, 2000), 185–95, at 195, as "mannered, opinionated and whimsically anti-Western."

9. Lucy Butler, ed., *Robert Byron: Letters Home* (London, 1991).

10. Humphrey Carpenter, *The Brideshead Generation: Evelyn Waugh and Friends* (London, 1989), 73, 15.

11. For the American Thomas Whittemore and the Byzantine Institute, see chapter 4. The travels of Byron and his friends took place only very shortly after the fall of Ottoman rule, the rise of Ataturk (with whom Whittemore developed a close connection), and the events of 1922–23; when he wrote *The*

Byzantine Achievement Byron had originally planned to write a history of the critical years 1919–23.

12. Fascinating details in Olivier Delouis, "Byzance sur la scène littéraire française," in *Byzance en Europe*, ed. Marie-France Auzépy (Saint-Denis: Presses Universitaires de Vincennes, 2003), 101–51; also on Theodora, Silvia Ronchey, "La 'femme fatale,' source d'une byzantinologie austère," ibid., 153–75.

13. The key elements about her in Procopius's *Wars* and *Secret History* relate to Theodora's early life and her performances in the Hippodrome at Constantinople, her imperiousness, her concern for repentant prostitutes, her support of eastern Monophysites, and the famous scene where Procopius claims that she prevented Justinian from running away during the Nika riot of 532 with the (borrowed) words "empire is a fine winding sheet." The historical Theodora, and especially the Monophysite tradition, are discussed in Volker-Lorenz Menze, *Justinian and the Making of the Syrian Orthodox Church* (Oxford, UK: Oxford University Press, 2008).

14. Steven Runciman, *History of the Crusades*, 3 vols. (Cambridge, UK: Cambridge University Press, 1951–54).

15. Peter Frankopan, *The First Crusade: The Call from the East* (London: Bodley Head, 2012), allows much more agency to Alexius.

16. Christopher Tyerman, *God's War: A New History of the Crusades* (London: Allen Lane, 2006), 553. For the Byzantine view see Angeliki E. Laiou, ed., *Urbs Capta: The Fourth Crusade and Its Consequences* (Paris: Lethielleux, 2005); Angeliki E. Laiou and Roy P. Mottahadeh, eds., *The Crusades from the Perspective of Byzantium and the Muslim World* (Washington, DC: Dumbarton Oaks, 2001); see also Christopher MacEvitt, *The Crusades and the Christian World of the East: Rough Tolerance* (Philadelphia: University of Pennsylvania Press, 2008), and some of the chapters in Jonathan Harris, Catherine Holmes, Eugenia Russell, eds., *Byzantines, Latins and Turks in the Eastern Mediterranean World after 1150* (Oxford, UK: Oxford University Press, 2013).

17. This applies even to some very distinguished editors of key Byzantine texts.

18. See for instance Tia M. Kolbaba, "On the Closing of the Churches and the Rebaptism of Latins: Greek Perfidy or Latin Slander?," *BMGS* 29, no. 1 (2005), 39–51.

19. Compare A. Papadakis, *Crisis in Byzantium: The Filioque Controversy in*

the Patriarchate of Gregory II of Cyprus (1283–1289), rev. ed. (Crestwood, NY: St. Vladimir's Seminary Press, 1996), especially his introduction, 1–14, at 7–9, and "Reflections," 200–208.

20. For instance Stefaan Neirynck, "Neilus Doxopatres's *Oeconomia Dei*," in *Byzantine Theologians*, ed. A. Rigo and P. Ermilov, Quaderni di *Nea Rhome* 3 (Rome: Università degli studi di Roma "Tor Vergata," 2009), 51–69.

21. Andrew F. Stone, "Nerses IV 'the Gracious,' Manuel I Komnenos, the Patriarch Michael Anchialos and Negotiations for Church Union between Byzantium and the Armenian Church, 1165–1173," *JÖB* 55 (2005), 191–208, at 101.

22. It is invidious to cite specific examples, but one cannot help but be struck to find in an important recent study of the iconoclast era (not, one notices, of "iconoclasm") the categorical statement that "Theology is not why iconoclasm happened": Leslie Brubaker and John F. Haldon, *Byzantium in the Iconoclast Era, ca. 680–850: A History* (Cambridge, UK: Cambridge University Press, 2011), 783. In contrast, according to Stone, "Nerses IV," 191, "Few areas of scholarship invite more animated discussion than theology. This discipline . . . cannot be avoided in the study of the Byzantine empire."

23. See Warren Treadgold, ed., *Renaissances before the Renaissance: Cultural Revivals of Late Antiquity and the Middle Ages* (Stanford, CA: Stanford University Press, 1984), 1–22.

24. There is intriguing information about the role of women patrons and collectors before and after 1453 in Donald M. Nicol, *The Byzantine Lady: Ten Portraits, 1250–1500* (Cambridge, UK: Cambridge University Press, 1994).

25. E. Fryde, *The Early Palaeologan Renaissance (1261–ca. 1360)* (Leiden: Brill, 2000); I. Ševčenko, "The Palaeologan Renaissance," in *Renaissances before the Renaissance*, ed. Treadgold, 144–71 (a revival, not a renaissance). Niels Gaul, *Thomas Magistros und die spätbyzantinische Sophistik. Studien zum Humanismus urbaner Eliten in der frühen Palaiologenzeit* (Wiesbaden: Harassowitz, 2001), especially 197–203, argues that it is better to avoid the term. For attempts to find traces of the Italian commune in late Byzantine Thessalonike, see John W. Barker, "Late Byzantine Thessalonike: A Second City's Challenges and Responses," *DOP* 57 (2003), 5–33, appendix B, 32–33; with J. Harris, "Constantinople as a City-State, ca. 1360–1453," in *Byzantines, Latins, and Turks*, ed. Harris, Holmes, and Russell, 119–40.

26. Ševčenko, "The Palaeologan Renaissance," 165.

27. Writing of the learned authors of the Palaeologan period, Niels Gaul aptly calls this elaborate literary Greek "an atticizing sociolect."

28. A well-known example is the inaugural lecture given by Cyril Mango in 1974 in the Bywater and Sotheby Chair of Byzantine and Modern Greek Language and Literature at Oxford: Cyril Mango, *Byzantine Literature as a Distorting Mirror* (Oxford, UK: Clarendon Press, 1975). Attempts to find "originality" in Byzantium: A. Littlewood, ed., *Originality in Byzantine Literature, Art and Music* (Oxford, UK: Oxbow, 1995); on the problem, S. Papaioannou, *Michael Psellos. Rhetoric and Authorship in Byzantium* (Cambridge, UK: Cambridge University Press, 2013), 20.

29. The classic statement is by H. Hunger, "On the Imitation (*Mimesis*) of Antiquity in Byzantine Literature," *DOP* 23/24 (1969/70), 17–38.

30. See I. Nilsson, "The Same Story, but Another: A Reappraisal of Literary Imitation in Byzantium," in *Imitatio, Aemulatio, Variatio*, ed. A. Rhoby and E. Schiffer, Akten des int. wiss. Symposions zur byzantinische Sprache und Literatur (Vienna, 2010), 195–208; and M. Mullett, "Imitatio-aemulatio-variatio," ibid., 279–82.

31. See Margaret Mullett, "No Drama, No Poetry, No Fiction, No Readership, No Literature," in *Companion to Byzantium*, ed. Liz James (Chichester, UK: Wiley-Blackwell, 2010), 227–38; despite p. 336, a substantial section titled "Reading Byzantine Texts" still ignores the theological writing that survives in such vast quantities. Mullett begins, "It used to be thought . . . ," but her rebuttal shows that these assumptions are by no means dead. Mary Whitby's contribution in the same volume ("Rhetorical Questions," 239–50) is an excellent short introduction to the overwhelming prominence of rhetorical elements in Byzantine literature, another feature that modern scholars find difficult.

32. Several recent publications deal with Byzantine humor, in literary texts (especially satire and parody) and more generally: for instance Shaun Tougher, "Having Fun in Byzantium," in *A Companion to Byzantium*, ed. James., chapter 11.

33. Warren Treadgold, *The Medieval Review*, 11.03.03.

34. Some ways forward are indicated by the contributors to the important volume *La face cachée de la littérature byzantine. Le texte en tant que message immédiat*, ed. P. Odorico, Actes du colloque international, Paris, en mémoire de Constantin Leventis, Dossiers byzantins 11 (Paris: Centre d'études byzantines,

neo-helléniques et sud-ouest européennes, École des Hautes Études en Sciences Sociales, 2012).

35. See G. Fatouros and M. Grünbart, eds., *Theatron: rhetorische Kultur in Spätantike und Mittelalter* (Berlin: de Gruyter, 2007).

36. Publications on Byzantine poetry are currently leading the way, though much attention has also been given to historiography and the novel. Floris Bernard, *Writing and Reading Byzantine Secular Poetry, 1025–1081* (Oxford: Oxford University Press, 2014) vividly portrays the explicitly competitive nature of literary production in this period; arguing for its "utilitarian quality," see Elizabeth M. Jeffreys, "Why Produce Verse in Twelfth-Century Constantinople?," in *Doux remède: Poésie et poétique à Byzance*, ed. P. Odorico, P. A. Agapitos, and M. Hinterberger, Acts of the Fourth International Philological Colloquium *Hermeneia* (Paris: Centre d'études byzantines, néo-helléniques et sud-ouest européennes, École des hautes études en sciences sociales, 2009), 219–28.

37. H. Hunger, *Die hochsprachliche profane Literatur der Byzantiner* (Munich: Verlag C. H. Beck, 1978). A new history of Byzantine literature by P. A. Agapitos is currently awaited. Alexander P. Kazhdan's two posthumous volumes, *A History of Byzantine Literature (650–850)*, in collaboration with Lee Sherry and Christine Angelidi (Athens: National Hellenic Research Foundation Institute for Byzantine Research, 1999), and *A History of Byzantine Literature (850–1000)*, ed. Christine Angelidi (Athens: National Hellenic Research Foundation Institute for Byzantine Research, 2006), do not extend beyond AD 1000, and take a firmly positivist view. See also P. Magdalino, "A History of Byzantine Literature for Historians," in *Pour une "nouvelle" histoire de la literature byzantine: problèmes, méthodes, approches, propositions*, P. Odorico and P. A. Agapitos (Paris: Centre d'Études byzantines, 2002), 167–84.

Chapter 2. Empire

1. Anthony Kaldellis, *Hellenism in Byzantium: The Transformations of Greek Identity and the Reception of the Classical Tradition* (Cambridge, UK: Cambridge University Press, 2007), on which see chapter 3; the same author's *Ethnography after Antiquity: Foreign Lands and Peoples in Byzantine Literature* (Phil-

adelphia: University of Pennsylvania Press, 2013), chapter 3, lays stress on references in Byzantine literature to the concept of *politeia* ("polity") in contrast to *basileia* ("empire"); and see Dimitris Krallis, "'Democratic' Action in Eleventh-Century Byzantium: Michael Attaleiates's 'Republicanism' in Context," *Viator* 40.2 (2009), 35–53.

2. Heraclius (610–41) was reported to entertain the idea of moving the capital to Carthage, and Constans II (641–68) briefly thought of Sicily, but even if credible, both ideas arose only in desperate moments.

3. Especially Peter Heather, *The Fall of the Roman Empire: A New History* (Basingstoke, UK: Macmillan, 2005); and Bryan Ward-Perkins, *The Fall of Rome and the End of Civilization* (Oxford, UK: Oxford University Press, 2005).

4. See the magisterial work by Chris Wickham, *Framing the Early Middle Ages: Europe and the Mediterranean, 400–800* (Oxford, UK: Oxford University Press, 2005); with Michael McCormick, *Origins of the European Economy: Communications and Commerce, AD 300–900* (Cambridge, UK: Cambridge University Press, 2001). McCormick returns to the theme in "Movements and Markets in the First Millennium: Information, Containers, and Shipwrecks," in *Trade and Markets in Byzantium*, ed. C. Morrisson (Washington, DC: Dumbarton Oaks, 2012), 51–98.

5. A. Giardina, "Esplosione di tardoantico," *Studi Storici* 40 (1999), 157–80; Eng. trans. in Averil Cameron, *Late Antiquity on the Eve of Islam* (Farnham, UK: Ashgate, 2013), no. I. Discussion of the periodization of late antiquity continues unabated, as can be seen for instance from the inclusion of four articles on the topic in the first issue in 2008 of the *Journal of Late Antiquity*.

6. Brent D. Shaw, "After Rome: Transformations of the Early Mediterranean World," *New Left Review* 51 (May/June 2008), 89–114, especially 112 (a review-discussion of Wickham, *Framing the Early Middle Ages*).

7. The network and publication series *Impact of Empire* (Leiden: Brill, 2001–) defines itself as ending in AD 476, the traditional date for the fall of the western empire. Johann P. Arnason and Kurt A. Raaflaub, eds., *The Roman Empire in Context: Historical and Comparative Perspectives* (Chichester, UK: Wiley-Blackwell, 2011), contains chapters by Garth Fowden on the long periodization of late antiquity and John Haldon on the eastern empire in the seventh and eighth centuries.

8. A provocative set of lectures on late antiquity refers to Justinian as cross-

ing "a Rubicon of Byzantine culture" (Polymnia Athanassiadi, *Vers la pensée unique. La montée de l'intolérance dans l'Antiquité tardive* [Paris: Belles Lettres, 2010], at 113).

9. The subject of a long series of books by Jack Goody and others, with the object of breaking down prevailing westernizing assumptions in historical scholarship. Most recently see Goody, *The Eurasian Miracle* (Cambridge, UK: Polity Press, 2010); with J. M. Hobson, *The Eastern Origins of Western Civilization* (Cambridge, UK: Cambridge University Press, 2004. For a Eurasian perspective relating to a later period see J. P. Arnason and B. Wittrock, eds., *Eurasian Transformations, Tenth to Thirteenth Centuries: Crystallizations, Divergences, Renaissances,* Medieval Encounters 10, no. 3 (Leiden: Brill, 2004).

10. Aziz al-Azmeh discusses the implications of Goody's argument for Islam in "Jack Goody and the Location of Islam," *Theory, Culture and Society* 26, nos. 7–8 (2009), 71–84; many of the points he makes can also be applied to the case of Byzantium.

11. Yet another strategy that has been tried is to assign Byzantium to an essentialist "Orthodox civilization" or "Orthodox sphere," neither fully eastern nor, certainly, western; see later and chapter 5.

12. David Abulafia and Nora Berend, eds., *Medieval Frontiers. Concepts and Practices* (Aldershot, UK: Ashgate, 2002).

13. See Susan E. Alcock, Terence N. D'Altroy, Kathleen D. Morrison, with Carla M. Sinopli, eds., *Empires: Perspectives from Archaeology and History* (Cambridge, UK: Cambridge University Press, 2001); for Rome and China see in particular Walter Scheidel, ed., *Rome and China: Comparative Perspectives on Ancient World Empires* (Oxford, UK: Oxford University Press, 2009). Ian Morris and Walter Scheidel, eds., *The Dynamics of Ancient Empires: From Assyria to Byzantium* (Stanford, CA: Stanford University Press, 2009), unusually includes a chapter on Byzantium, by John Haldon: "The Byzantine Empire," 205–52, but there is no equivalent chapter in Peter Fibiger Bang and C. A. Bayly, eds., *Tributary Empires in Global History*, Cambridge Imperial and Post-Colonial Studies (Basingstoke, UK: Palgrave Macmillan, 2011). For the "American empire" see Niall Ferguson's *Colossus: The Rise and Fall of the American Empire* (London: Penguin, 2005); with Cullen Murphy, *Are We Rome? The End of an Empire and the Fate of America* (Boston: Houghton Mifflin Co., 2007). Both

these current historiographical trends are discussed in detail by Phiroze Vasunia, "The Comparative Study of Empires," *JRS* 101 (2011), 222–37.

14. "The Byzantine Empire," 206–8.

15. Edward Luttwak, *The Grand Strategy of the Byzantine Empire* (Cambridge, MA: Belknap Press of Harvard University Press, 2009), which appeared in the same year as a collection of essays, also containing a section on Byzantium, with the title *The Virtual American Empire: War, Faith and Power* (New Brunswick, NJ:Transaction Books, 2009). For Rome see Luttwak's earlier book, *The Grand Strategy of the Roman Empire from the First Century AD to the Third* (Baltimore: Johns Hopkins University Press, 1976). *A Grand Strategy of the Soviet Union*, also by Luttwak, appeared in 1983 (London: Weidenfeld and Nicolson).

16. See further Averil Cameron, "Thinking with Byzantium," *Transactions of the Royal Historical Society*, 21 (2011), 39–57.

17. See Dimiter Angelov, *Imperial Ideology and Political Thought in Byzantium, 1204–1330* (Cambridge, UK: Cambridge University Press, 2007).

18. See Jack A. Goldstone and John F. Haldon, "Ancient States, Empires and Exploitation: Problems and Perspectives," in *Dynamics of Ancient Empires*, ed. Morris and Scheidel, 3–29; John F. Haldon, *The State and the Tributary Mode of Production* (London: Verso, 1993). Thomas J. Barfield, "The Shadow Empires: Imperial State Formation along the Chinese-Nomad Frontier," in *Empires*, ed. Alcock et al., 10–41, at 28–39.

19. John F. Haldon, "Comparative State Formation: The Later Roman Empire in the Wider World," in *The Oxford Handbook of Late Antiquity*, ed. Scott Fitzgerald Johnson (Oxford, UK: Oxford University Press, 2012), 1111–47, at 1124.

20. See the essays in Lucy Grig and Gavin Kelly, *Two Romes: Rome and Constantinople in Late Antiquity* (Oxford, UK: Oxford University Press, 2012).

21. John Haldon is one of the relatively few Byzantine historians who have been concerned with the question of elites and social macrostructures; see on the early period "The Fate of the Late Roman Senatorial Elite: Extinction or Transformation?" in *Elites Old and New in the Byzantine and Early Islamic Near East*, ed. John Haldon and Lawrence I. Conrad, The Byzantine and Early Islamic Near East VI (Princeton, NJ: Darwin Press, 2004), 179–234; and for later periods, John F. Haldon, *Byzantium: A History* (Stroud, UK: Tempus, 2000), 117–30.

22. See on this N. Oikonomides, "The Role of the State in the Economy," in *The Economic History of Byzantium* 3, ed. Angeliki E. Laiou (Washington, DC: Dumbarton Oaks, 2002), 973–1058, at 990–1019.

23. For the landowning power-base see J.-C. Cheynet, *Pouvoir et contestations à Byzance (963–1210)* (Paris: Publications de la Sorbonne, 1990). On the question of whether Byzantium had an aristocracy see Paul Magdalino, "Court Society and Aristocracy," in *A Social History of Byzantium*, ed. John F. Haldon (Chichester, UK: Wiley-Blackwell, 2009), 212–32, especially 218–30; and Paul Stephenson, "The Rise of the Middle Byzantine Aristocracy and the Decline of the Imperial State," in *The Byzantine World*, ed. Paul Stephenson (London: Routledge, 2010), 22–33 (for the period 950–1204).

24. Peter Sarris, " Economics, Trade and 'Feudalism,'" in *A Companion to Byzantium*, ed. Liz James (Chichester, UK: Wiley-Blackwell, 2010), 25–42; with id., *Economy and Society in the Age of Justinian* (Cambridge, UK: Cambridge University Press, 2006).

25. Names can be extremely misleading, but major advances have been made as a result of detailed prosopographical work by British and German research teams.

26. Haldon, "The Byzantine Empire," 205; having stated that the case of Byzantium is anomalous, he concentrates in his chapter on its modes of exploitation and state structures.

27. Ibid., 251–52, citing the work of Gary Runciman.

28. Barfield, "The Shadow Empires," 29–33.

29. Dimitri Obolensky, *The Byzantine Commonwealth: Eastern Europe, 500–1453* (London: Weidenfeld and Nicolson, 1971); cf. Garth Fowden's *Empire to Commonwealth: Consequences of Monotheism in Late Antiquity* (Princeton, NJ: Princeton University Press, 1993); and for the post-Byzantine period, Paschalis Kitromilides, *An Orthodox Commonwealth: Symbolic Legacies and Cultural Encounters in Southeastern Europe* (Aldershot, UK: Ashgate, 2007).

30. *Empire to Commonwealth*, 165–68, 169. Islam is also part of Fowden's conception: G. Fowden, "The Umayyad Horizon," *JRA* 25 (2012), 974–82; and id., *Before and After Muhammad* (Princeton, NJ: Princeton University Press, 2013).

31. C. Raffensperger, "Revisiting the Idea of the Byzantine Commonwealth," *Byzantinische Forschungen* 28 (2004), 159–74; Evelyne Patlagean, *Un*

Moyen Âge grec. Byzance IXe–XIVe siècle (Paris: Albin Michel, 2007), 387; J. P. Arnason, "Byzantium and Historical Sociology," in *The Byzantine World*, ed. P. Stephenson (London: Routledge, 2010), 491–504, at 503–504.

32. For which see J. H. Elliott, *History in the Making* (New Haven, CT: Yale University Press, 2012), 211–12.

33. See Jonathan Shepard, "Byzantium's Overlapping Circles," in *Proceedings of the 21st International Congress of Byzantine Studies, London, 21–26 August 2006*, I, *Plenary Papers*, ed. Elizabeth Jeffreys (Aldershot, UK: Ashgate, 2006), 15–55; id., "The Byzantine Commonwealth, 1000–1550," in *Cambridge History of Christianity* V, ed. M. Angold (Cambridge, UK: Cambridge University Press, 2006), 3–52.

34. Arnason, "Byzantium and Historical Sociology."

35. "Emperors and Expansionism: From Rome to Middle Byzantium," in *Medieval Frontiers*, ed. Abulafia and Berend, 55–82.

36. G. Ostrogorski, *Geschichte des byzantinischen Staates* (Munich: Beck, 1940); Eng. trans. by Joan Hussey, *History of the Byzantine State* (Oxford, UK: Oxford University Press, 1956). Consultation of the catalogue of the Bodleian Library in Oxford brings up eight copies of the various German and English editions.

37. Judith Herrin, *Byzantium: The Surprising Life of a Medieval Empire* (London: Allen Lane, 2007); Patlagean, *Un Moyen Âge grec: Byzance*; cf. Patlagean, "Byzance dans le millénaire médiéval," *Annales HSS* LX, no. 4 (2005), 721–29. On Ostrogorsky see Patlagean, *Un Moyen Âge grec*, 49–51; and Arnason, "Byzantium and Historical Sociology," 495–98.

38. Among key Byzantine sites is Amorium in Anatolia, where excavation began in 1987 and reached its twenty-fifth year in 2012, while current work at Sagalassos and Euchaita focuses on the relation of urban sites and their hinterlands; survey archaeology not specifically aimed at the Byzantine period increasingly takes a wide diachronic approach with important results for questions of settlement and economic levels. Peter Thonemann, *The Meander Valley: A Historical Geography from Antiquity to Byzantium* (Cambridge, UK: Cambridge University Press, 2011), is an outstanding example of a longitudinal study.

39. Marlia Mundell Mango, *Byzantine Trade, 4th–12th Centuries: The Archaeology of Local, Regional and International Exchange* (Farnham, UK: Ashgate,

2009); C. Morrisson, ed., *Trade and Markets in Byzantium* (Washington, DC: Dumbarton Oaks, 2012). The work of David Abulafia, Michel Balard, and others puts Byzantium into the context of Mediterranean and other trade, especially from the twelfth century onward (see also D. Abulafia, "Venetian Commercial Expansion in the Eastern Mediterranean, 8th–11th Centuries," in *Byzantine Trade*, ed. Mango, 371–91).

40. For instance the authors of the important chapter on the sixth century are respectively a numismatist and an archaeologist: Cécile Morrisson and Jean-Pierre Sodini, "The Sixth-Century Economy, Background," in *Economic History of Byzantium* 1, ed. Angeliki E Laiou (Washington DC: Dumbarton Oaks, 2002), 171–220.

41. J.-C. Cheynet, *La société byzantine: l'apport des sceaux*, Bilans de recherché 3 (Paris: Association des amis du Centre d'histoire et civilisation de Byzance, 2008), 2 vols., and the series Studies in Byzantine Sigillography are basic guides.

42. For which see J.-M. Carrié, "Were Late Roman and Byzantine Economies Market Economies? A Comparative Look at Historiography," in *Trade and Markets in Byzantium*, ed. Morrisson, 13–26. M. Hendy, *Studies in the Byzantine Monetary Economy, ca. 300–1450* (Cambridge, UK: Cambridge University Press, 1985) exemplifies the primitivist approach.

43. Gilbert Dagron, *L'hippodrome de Constantinople. Jeux, people et politique* (Paris: Éditions de Gallimard, 2011), 340, a brilliant exposition.

44. The idea that Byzantine emperors controlled the church ("caesaropapism") is effectively addressed by Gilbert Dagron, *Emperor and Priest: The Imperial Office in Byzantium*, Eng. trans. (Cambridge, UK: Cambridge University Press, 2003), even if he may overstate the sense in which they themselves were seen as priestly; see also Arnason, "Byzantium and Historical Sociology," 498–500.

45. Though to see it as particularly tolerant goes too far: see chapter 5.

Chapter 3. Hellenism

1. Cyril Mango, *Byzantium: The Empire of New Rome* (London: Weidenfeld and Nicolson, 1980).

2. See on this Despina Christodoulou, "Byzantium in Nineteenth-Century Greek Historiography," in *The Byzantine World*, ed. Paul Stephenson (London: Routledge, 2010), 445–61.

3. Though one can see road signs in northern Greece pointing to "Constantinople." The dream of recovering Hagia Sophia in Istanbul survives even now, against Turkish calls to reopen it for Muslim prayer.

4. Peter Mackridge, "The Heritages of the Modern Greeks," *The British Academy Review* 19 (2012), 33–41, a lecture given in 2011 for the 125th anniversary of the British School at Athens.

5. These issues can be conveniently followed in several chapters in Stephenson, ed., *The Byzantine World*: see Paul Stephenson, "The World of Byzantine Studies," 429–33; Diether Roderich Reinsch, "The History of Editing Byzantine Historiographical Texts," 435–44; Srdan Pirivatric, "A Case Study in the Emergence of Byzantine Studies: Serbia in the Nineteenth and Twentieth Centuries," 481–90; Paul Stephenson, "Pioneers of Popular Byzantine History: Freeman, Gregorovius, Schlumberger," 462–80.

6. Ironically, the Koraes Chair itself was founded in 1918 with the strong support of Venizelos and in the most optimistic phase of the "great idea." It is remarkable that the scandal caused by the anti-Greek war reporting of its first incumbent, Arnold Toynbee, did not completely undermine the support of the College authorities for the chair (which still exists).

7. R. H. Jenkins, "The Hellenistic Origins of Byzantine Literature," *DOP* 17 (1963), 39–52, at 29. A similar view is found in *Byzantium: The Empire of New Rome* (London: Weidenfeld and Nicolson, 1980), by Cyril Mango, himself a past holder of the Koraes Chair.

8. Mackridge, "The Heritages of the Modern Greeks," 34. For the modern Greek reception of Byzantium see M. Lassiothiotakis, "Une Grèce chrétienne. Les lettrés grecs et la réhabilitation de Byzance sans la seconde moitié du XIXe siècle," in *Présence de Byzance. Textes réunis par Jean-Michel Spieser* (Lausanne: Infolio, 2007), 91–112, 174–82.

9. On Greek and eastern European scholarship on Byzantium in this regard see the contributions of D. Kyrtatas and S. Ćurčič in *Nea Hestia*, July–Aug. 2008, 138–47, and Sept. 2008, 492–500; with G. Grivaud, ed., *Les mishellénismes*, Actes du séminaire organisé à l'Ecole française d'Athènes, 16–18 mars 1998 (Athens: Ecole française d'Athènes, 2001).

10. The important role of Thessalonike in Byzantine cultural and intellectual life in the thirteenth and fourteenth centuries is also very clear, though so also is the frequency with which its intellectuals and churchmen gravitated to the imperial center at Constantinople.

11. Florin Curta, *The Edinburgh History of the Greeks, ca. 500–1050: The Early Middle Ages* (Edinburgh: Edinburgh University Press, 2011), deals with these issues.

12. See for instance G. Prinzing and Maciej Salamon, with Paul Stephenson, eds., *Byzantium and East Central Europe*, Byzantina et Slavica Cracoviensia 3 (Cracow: "Historia Jagellonica," Jagiellonian University, 2010).

13. See Scott Fitzgerald Johnson, ed., *Languages and Cultures of Eastern Christianity: Greek*, The Worlds of Eastern Christianity, 300–1500, eds. Robert G. Hoyland and Arietta Papaconstantinou (Farnham, UK: Ashgate, 2014).

14. See G.W.Bowersock, *Hellenism in Late Antiquity* (Ann Arbor: University of Michigan Press, 1990); id., *Mosaics as History: The Near East from Late Antiquity to Islam* (Cambridge, MA: Belknap Press of Harvard University Press, 2006); id.,"Reconsidering Hellenism in the Roman Near East," in *The Sculptural Environment of the Roman Near East: Reflections on Culture, Ideology, and Power*, ed. Yaron Z. Elias, Elise A. Friedland, and Sharon Herbert (Leuven: Peeters, 2008), 21–23.

15. "Unholy and loathsome" according to the sixth-century *Codex Justinianus*: see N. Siniossoglou, *Plato and Theodoret: The Christian Appropriation of Platonic Philosophy and the Hellenic Intellectual Resistance* (Cambridge, UK: Cambridge University Press, 2008), 47, on which see later in this chapter.

16. The shift is discussed for instance by Dimiter Angelov, "Byzantine Ideological Reactions to the Latin Conquest of Constantinople," in *Urbs Capta: The Fourth Crusade and Its Consequences*, ed. Angeliki E. Laiou (Paris: Lethielleux, 2005), 293–310, at 300–302; whether this is an indicator of "protonationalism" is a moot point, on which see R. Beaton, "Antique Nation? Hellenes on the Eve of Greek Independence and in Twelfth-Century Byzantium," *BMGS* 11, no. 1 (2007), 76–95.

17. Patrick Leigh Fermor, *Roumeli: Travels in Northern Greece* (London: John Murray, 1966), 106–7.

18. See further Averil Cameron, "The Absence of Byzantium," *Nea Hestia*, Jan. 2008, 4–59; and cf. Christoph Markschies, "Does It Make Sense to Speak

about a 'Hellenization of Christianity' in Antiquity?," *Church History and Religious Culture* 92.1 (2012), 5–34.

19. Rowan Williams, *Sobornost* 2, no. 1 (1980), 72; see Aaron P. Johnson, "Hellenism and Its Discontents," in *The Oxford Handbook of Late Antiquity*, ed. Scott Fitzgerald Johnson (Oxford, UK/New York: Oxford University Press, 2012), 437–66; "toolbox," ibid., 439; id., "Philosophy, Hellenicity, Law: Porphyry on Origen, Again," *JHS* 132 (2012), 55–69; A. Perrot, ed., *Les chrétiens et l'hellénisme: identités religieuses et culture grecque dans l'Antiquité tardive* (Paris: Éditions Rue d'Ulm/Presses de l'École Normale Supérieure, 2012).

20. Several works by Judith Lieu are indicative and important: for instance *Neither Jew nor Greek? Constructing Early Christianity* (London: T. and T. Clark, 2002); *Christian Identity in the Jewish and Graeco-Roman World* (Oxford, UK: Oxford University Press, 2004).

21. P. Athanassiadi, *Julian and Hellenism: An Intellectual Biography* (Oxford, UK: Clarendon Press, 1981); the term "Hellenism" was dropped in the title of the revised edition of 1992.

22. See Peter Brown, *Power and Persuasion in Late Antiquity: Towards a Christian Empire* (Madison: Wisconsin University Press, 1992); with Susanna Elm, *Sons of Hellenism, Fathers of the Church: Emperor Julian, Gregory of Nazianzus and the Vision of Rome* (Berkeley: University of California Press, 2012); Siniossoglou, *Plato and Theodoret*, 56–61.

23. Anthony Kaldellis, *Hellenism in Byzantium: The Transformations of Greek Identity and the Reception of the Classical Greek Tradition* (Cambridge, UK: Cambridge University Press, 2007); Kaldellis offers a pugnacious but unconvincing defense of his views in "From Rome to New Rome, from Empire to Nation State: Reopening the Question of Byzantium's Roman Identity," in *Two Romes. Rome and Constantinople in Late Antiquity*, ed. Lucy Grig and Gavin Kelly (Oxford, UK: Oxford University Press, 387–404.

24. *Hellenism in Byzantium*, 118, cf. for example, 63, 83.

25. Anthony Kaldellis, *The Argument of Psellos' Chronographia* (Leiden: Brill, 1999); *Procopius of Caesarea: Tyranny, History, and Philosophy at the End of Antiquity* (Philadelphia: University of Pennsylvania Press, 2004); "The Historical and Religious Views of Agathias: A Reinterpretation," *Byzantion* 69 (1999), 206–52; "The Religion of Ioannes Lydos," *Phoenix* 57 (2003), 300–316; "Identi-

fying Dissident Circles in Sixth-Century Byzantium: The Friendship of Prokopios and Ioannes Lydos," *Florilegium* 21 (2004), 1–17. Psellus's Hellenism is discussed in literary terms by S. Papaioannou, *Michael Psellos: Rhetoric and Authorship in Byzantium* (Cambridge, UK: Cambridge University Press, 2013), chapter 5.

26. N. Siniossoglou, *Radical Platonism in Byzantium: Illumination and Utopia in Gemistos Plethon* (Cambridge, UK: Cambridge University Press, 2011).

27. For the idea that Hellenism "failed" in late antiquity see Kaldellis, *Hellenism in Byzantium*, 166–71.

28. Termed by Elizabeth A. Clark "the new intellectual history": ead., *History, Theory, Text: Historians and the Linguistic Turn* (Cambridge, MA: Harvard University Press, 2004), 106–29, 159.

29. For a somewhat provocative discussion of "late antiquity" as seen by the Byzantines themselves see Stratis Papaioannou, "The Byzantine Late Antiquity," in *A Companion to Late Antiquity*, ed. Philip Rousseau (Chichester, UK: Wiley-Blackwell, 2009), 17–28, arguing for a specifically late antique aesthetic passed on to Byzantium. The idea is intriguing but begs the question of what is Byzantine and what late antique; space has not allowed the more detailed discussion of late antiquity the author's argument would need in order to be persuasive.

30. To confuse the issue further, it is also still sometimes described as the late Roman empire.

31. Johnson, "Hellenism and Its Discontents," 440–42; for Sophronius see also Phil Booth, *Crisis of Empire: Doctrine and Dissent at the End of Antiquity*, Transformation of the Classical Heritage 52 (Berkeley: University of California Press, 2013). Maximus Confessor, among the greatest of Orthodox theologians and author of many theological writings in Greek, also came from the milieu of Palestinian monasticism and traveled to Carthage, Constantinople, and Rome.

32. Some examples: Andrew S. Jacobs, *Remains of the Jews: The Holy Land and Christian Empire in Late Antiquity* (Stanford, CA: Stanford University Press, 2004); Isabella Sandwell, *Religious Identity in Late Antiquity: Greeks, Jews and Christians in Antioch* (Cambridge, UK: Cambridge University Press, 2007); Greg Fisher, *Between Empires: Arabs, Romans and Sasanians in Late Antiquity*

(Oxford, UK: Oxford University Press, 2011); many recent articles by Fergus Millar and Robert Hoyland deal with these issues in relation to Greek, Syriac, Arabs, and Arabic, and see also Philip Wood, ed., *History and Identity in the Late Antique East (500–1000)* (New York: Oxford University Press, 2012), and see Angelos Chaniotis, "European Identity: Learning from the Past?," in *Applied Classics: Comparisons, Constructs, Controversies*, ed. Angelos Chaniotis, Annika Kuhn, and Christina Kuhn, Heidelberger Althistorische Beiträge und Epigraphische Studien 46 (Munich: Franz Steiner Verlag, 2008), 27–56. Gill Page, *Being Byzantine: Greek Identity before the Ottomans* (Cambridge, UK: Cambridge University Press, 2008), takes up some of these themes in relation to late Byzantium.

33. One must except some works on the Latin empire, and studies of art in the Crusader kingdoms, for instance Lucy-Anne Hunt, *Byzantium, Eastern Christendom and Islam: Art at the Crossroads of the Medieval Mediterranean*, 2 vols. (London: Pindar Press, 1998, 2000). I also very much regret that this book does not cover Byzantine-Islamic interactions, though that is a huge subject in itself; but see Helen C. Evans with Brandie Ratliff, eds., *Byzantium and Islam: Age of Transition, 7th–9th Century* (New Haven, CT: Yale University Press, 2012), the catalogue of an important recent exhibition.

34. See the controversial book by Alfred Gell, *Art and Agency: An Anthropological Theory* (Oxford, UK: Clarendon Press, 1998), with, for example, Robin Osborne and Jeremy Tanner, eds., *Art's Agency and Art History* (Oxford, UK: Blackwell, 2007).

35. See chapter 4.

36. Kaldellis, *Hellenism in Byzantium*, 137.

37. Ibid.

38. For earlier scholarship see C. M. Woodhouse, *Gemistos Plethon: Last of the Hellenes* (Oxford, UK: Clarendon Press, 1986), with translations of some of Plethon's works.

39. Siniossoglou, *Radical Platonism*, 39.

40. "The question of Hellenic continuity and identity in late antiquity is essentially a philosophical problem. . . . This crucial link between Hellenic identity and philosophy that Theodoret exploited is reaffirmed and verified in the fifteenth century by Plethon" *Plato and Theodoret*, 238–39.

41. Ibid., 237.

42. *Radical Platonism*, epilogue, 418–26, with 415; and cf. L. Bargeliotis, "The Enlightenment of the Hellenic 'genos' from Plethon to Vulgaris," *Skepsis* 20 (2009), 44–61.

43. See G. Karamanolis, "Plethon and Scholarios on Aristotle," in *Byzantine Philosophy and Its Ancient Sources*, ed. K. Ierodiakonou (Oxford, UK: Clarendon Press, 2002), 253–82.

44. Eng. trans. in Woodhouse, *Gemistos Plethon*, 192–214.

45. Siniossoglou attempts to deal with this (though with difficulty) in *Radical Platonism*, 125–34.

46. Woodhouse, *Gemistos Plethon*, 136, 167; for recent attempts to play down Plethon's paganism see *Radical Platonism*, 148–50.

47. A. D. Angelou, "Who Am I? Scholarios's Answer and Hellenic Identity," in *Philhellen: Studies in Honour of Robert Browning*, ed. C. N. Constantinides, N. M. Panagiotakis, and E. Jeffreys (Venice: Istituto ellenico di studi bizantini e postbizantini di Venezia, 1996), 1–19. C. Livanos, "The Conflict between Scholarios and Plethon: Religion and Communal Identity in Early Modern Greece," in *Modern Greek Literature. Critical Essays*, ed. G. Nagy and A. Stavrakopoulou, with J. Reilly (New York and London: Routledge, 2003), 24–41, defends Scholarios.

48. J. Monfasani "Pletho's Date of Death and the Burning of His Laws," *Byzantinische Zeitschrift* 98, no. 2 (2005), 459–63.

49. For doubts about Siniossoglou's essentialism see also K. Ierodiakonou, "Byzantine Philosophy Revisited (a Decade After)," in *The Many Faces of Byzantine Philosophy*, ed. K. Ierodiakonou (Athens: Norwegian Institute at Athens, 2012), 1–22, at 6–7.

50. G. Dagron, "Byzance et la Grèce antique: un impossible retour aux sources," in *La Grèce antique sous le regard du Moyen Âge occidental*, Cahiers de la Villa "Kerylos" 16, ed. J. Leclant and M. Zink (Paris: Boccard, 2005), 195–206, at 195.

51. Dagron, ibid., 203–4.

52. Hélène Ahrweiler, *L'idéologie politique de l'empire byzantine* (Paris: Presses Universitaires de France, 1975).; cf. ead., "The Hellenic Europe: Problems of Greek Continuity," in *The Making of Europe: Lectures and Studies* (Athens: Nea Synora Livanis Publishing Organization, 2000).

53. Averil Cameron, *The Byzantines* (Oxford, UK: Blackwell, 2006), 164–65, 167–68, also on the concept of nationalism or proto-nationalism.

54. See Millar, *A Greek Roman Empire*; Latin remained in use for some purposes even after the sixth century, but few Byzantines knew or read it until a much later period.

55. From the large literature see especially Tim Whitmarsh, *Greek Literature and the Roman Empire: The Politics of Imitation* (Oxford, UK: Oxford University Press, 2001); id., *The Second Sophistic* (Oxford, UK: Oxford University Press, 2005); Simon Swain, *Hellenism and Empire: Language, Classicism and Power in the Greek World, AD 50–250* (Oxford, UK: Clarendon Press, 1996).

56. Mango, *Byzantium: The Empire of New Rome*, 26, cited in *The Byzantines*, 15, in a discussion of Byzantine identity, ibid., 15–19.

Chapter 4. The Realms of Gold

1. B. V. Pentcheva, *The Sensual Icon. Space, Ritual and the Senses in Byzantium* (University Park: Pennsylvania State University Press, 2010), 127 and 7.

2. On which see Amalia G. Kakissis, "The Byzantine Research Fund Archive: Encounters of Arts and Crafts Architects in Byzantium," in *Scholars, Travels, Archives. Greek History and Culture through the British School at Athens*, ed. Michael Llewellyn Smith, Paschalis M. Kitromilides, and Eleni Calligas, British School at Athens Studies 17 (London: British School at Athens, 2009), 125–44.

3. A milestone was reached in 1852 by the publication of an album of lithographs by G. Fossati, *Aya Sofia, Constantinople* (London), with W. Salzenberg, *Alt-christliche Baudenkmale von Constantinopel vom V. bis XII. Jahrhundert* (Berlin, 1854).

4. Annabel Wharton, "Westminster Cathedral: Medieval Architectures and Religious Difference," *Journal of Medieval and Early Modern Studies* 26, no. 3 (1996), 523–57.

5. O. M. Dalton, *Byzantine Art and Archaeology* (Oxford, UK: Clarendon Press, 1911); see Christopher Entwhistle, "O. M. Dalton: 'Ploughing the Byzantine Furrow,'" in *Through the Looking Glass. Byzantium through British Eyes*,

ed. Robin Cormack and Elizabeth Jeffreys (Aldershot, UK: Variorum 2000), 177–83.

6. Byron was also a friend of the Mitford sisters, especially Nancy, and Diana Mitford married his friend Bryan Guinness.

7. Robert Byron, *The Byzantine Achievement: An Historical Perspective, AD 330–1453* (London: G. Routledge and Sons Ltd, 1929), author's note.

8. Robert Byron, *The Station* (London: Phoenix, 1928), 136.

9. For gold in Byzantine art see Rico Franses, "When All That Is Gold Does Not Glitter: On the Strange History of Looking at Byzantine Art," in *Icon and Word: The Power of Images in Byzantium. Studies Presented to Robin Cormack*, ed. Antony Eastmond and Liz James (Aldershot, UK: Ashgate, 2003), 13–23.

10. Procopius, *Buildings* I.1.1–78, on which see Paolo Cesaretti and Maria Luigia Fobelli, *Procopius di Cesarea, Santa Sofia di Costantinopoli. Un tempio di luce* (Milan: Jaca Book, 2011); marble: Liz James, *Light and Colour in Byzantine Art* (Oxford, UK: Oxford University Press, 1996), 116, on Paul the Silentiary and Constantine the Rhodian.

11. Henry Maguire and Eunice Dautermann Maguire are two scholars who have done much to bring out the secular side of Byzantine art: see Henry Maguire, "The Profane Aesthetic in Byzantine Art and Literature," *DOP* 53 (1999), 189–205; and especially Henry Maguire, "Unofficial Art and the Resistance to Orthodoxy," in *The Byzantine World*, ed. Paul Stephenson (London: Routledge, 2010), 320–33; Eunice Dautermann Maguire and Henry Maguire, *Other Icons: Art and Power in Byzantine Secular Culture* (Princeton, NJ: Princeton University Press, 2007); Henry Maguire, *Nectar and Illusion: Nature in Byzantine Art and Literature* (New York: Oxford University Press, 2012).

12. The early-seventh-century suite of silver dishes found in Cyprus and known as the David plates has often been attributed to the emperor Heraclius (610–41), but for a wealthy individual as the patron see Ruth Leader, "The David Plates Revisited: Transforming the Secular in Early Byzantium," *Art Bulletin* 82, no. 3 (2000), 407–27; the treasure is now divided between Cyprus and the Metropolitan Museum of Art, New York. Early Byzantine silver: Marlia Mundell Mango, *Silver from Early Byzantium: The Kaper Koraon and Related Treasures* (Baltimore: Walters Art Gallery, 1986); ivory (including late antique official diptychs and Middle Byzantine ivory caskets): Anthony Cutler, *The*

Craft of Ivory: Sources, Techniques and Uses in the Mediterranean World, AD 200–1450 (Washington, DC: Dumbarton Oaks, 1985); id., *The Hand of the Master. Craftsmanship, Ivory and Society in Byzantium, 9th–11th Centuries* (Princeton, NJ: Princeton University Press, 1994). To these categories one should add that of textiles, especially silks, imported by the west and much favored as royal gifts.

13. Gilbert Dagron, *Décrire et peindre. Essai sur le portrait iconique* (Paris: Gallimard, 2007), 7.

14. Anthony Eastmond discusses the difficulties of deciding what counts as "Byzantine" art, given the changing shape of the Byzantine state, and the coverage of some recent exhibitions, in "The Limits of Byzantine Art," in *A Companion to Byzantium*, ed. Liz James (Chichester, UK: Wiley-Blackwell, 2010), 313–22.

15. See James, *Light and Colour*, 118–23 and chapter 7; Robert S. Nelson, ed., *Visuality before and beyond the Renaissance: Seeing as Others Saw* (Cambridge, UK: Cambridge University Press, 2000).

16. Glenn Peers, "Object Relations: Theorizing the Late Antique Viewer," in *The Oxford Handbook of Late Antiquity*, ed. Scott Fitzgerald Johnson (New York: Oxford University Press, 2012), 970–93, at 973–74 (I am not sure I agree with the overall argument of the chapter).

17. A development of the early Byzantine period according to E. Kitzinger, *Byzantine Art in the Making: Main Lines of Stylistic Development in Mediterranean Art, 3rd–7th Century* (London: Faber, 1977).

18. As well as for a type of icon associated with the feast, like the early fifteenth-century example in the British Museum (see figure 9).

19. Michael Squire, *Image and Text in Graeco-Roman Antiquity* (Cambridge, UK: Cambridge University Press, 2009).

20. Brought out by Charles Barber, *Figure and Likeness: On the Limits of Representation in Byzantine Iconoclasm* (Princeton, NJ: Princeton University Press, 2002).

21. Even if not to the extent envisaged in the many publications on the subject by the late Paul Speck.

22. Kathleen Corrigan, *Visual Polemics in the Ninth-Century Byzantine Psalters* (Cambridge, UK: Cambridge University Press, 1992).

23. See especially Leslie Brubaker and John F. Haldon, *Byzantium in the*

Iconoclast Era, ca. 680–850: A History (Cambridge, UK: Cambridge University Press, 2011).

24. Matthew Dal Santo, *Debating the Saints' Cult in the Age of Gregory the Great* (Oxford, UK: Oxford University Press, 2012); with Peter Sarris, Matthew Dal Santo, and Phil Booth, eds., *An Age of Saints? Power, Conflict and Dissent in Early Medieval Christianity* (Leiden: Brill, 2011). The issue is also raised by Dirk Krausmüller, "God or Angels as Impersonators of Saints: A Belief in Its Context in the *Refutation* of Eustratius of Constantinople and in the Writings of Anastasius of Sinai," *Golden Horn* 2 (1998/99), available at http://www.isidore-of-seville.com/goudenhoorn/62dirk.html, accessed 05.09.2013; and especially by Gilbert Dagron, "'L'ombre d'un doute': l'hagiographie en question, VIe–XIe siècle," *DOP* 46 (1992), 59–68. The question did not go away: see Dirk Krausmüller, "Being, Seeming and Becoming: Patriarch Methodius on Divine Impersonation of Angels and Souls and the Origenist Alternative," *BZ* 79 (2009), 168–207, and "Denying Mary's Real Presence in Apparitions and Icons: Divine Impersonation in the Tenth-Century *Life* of Constantine the Ex-Jew," *Byzantion* 78 (2008), 281–303.

25. Question 89 (19), *PG* 89.717C; cf. Krausmüller, "God or Angels."

26. For the latter, Henry Maguire, *The Icons of Their Bodies. Saints and Their Images in Byzantium* (Princeton, NJ: Princeton University Press, 1996), 12–13.

27. Anna Kartsonis, *Anastasis: The Making of an Image* (Princeton, NJ: Princeton University Press, 1986), 40–63; Averil Cameron, "The Language of Images," in *The Church and the Arts*, ed. Diana Wood, Studies in Church History 28 (Oxford, UK: Blackwell, 1992), 1–42.

28. See Gilbert Dagron, "Holy Images and Likeness," *DOP* 45 (1991), 23–33.

29. See Corrigan, *Visual Polemics*. Hostility to images in the eighth century has been seen in modern scholarship as a response to the purist stance of Islam, but it is Jews who were the target in portrayals in Byzantine visual art.

30. As I argued in "Blaming the Jews: The Seventh-Century Invasions of Palestine in Context," *TM* 14 (*Mélanges Gilbert Dagron*) (2002), 57–78.

31. Corrigan, *Visual Polemics*, 32.

32. L. Brubaker, "Critical Approaches to Art History," in *The Oxford Handbook of Byzantine Studies*, ed. Elizabeth Jeffreys, with J. Haldon and R. Cormack (Oxford, UK: Oxford University Press, 2008), 59–66, at 63.

33. Liz James, "Art and Text in Byzantium," in *Art and Text in Byzantine*

Culture, ed. L. James (Cambridge, UK: Cambridge University Press, 2007), 1–12, at 1.

34. Ibid., 3, 7; see also Henry Maguire, *Art and Eloquence in Byzantium* (Princeton, NJ: Princeton University Press, 1981); and id., "Metaphors of Religion in Byzantine Literature and Art," in *Imitatio, Aemulatio, Variatio*, ed. A. Rhoby and E. Schiffer, Akten des int. wiss. Symposions zur byzantinische Sprache und Literatur (Vienna, 2010), 189–94.

35. The writing and function of epigrams in Middle Byzantium (many on visual art) currently constitute a growing field, and *ekphrasis* has also attracted a large literature: see Ruth Webb, "Ekphrasis Ancient and Modern: The Invention of a Genre," *Word and Image* 15 (1999), 7–18; Jaś Elsner, "Introduction: The Genres of *Ekphrasis*," *Ramus* 31 (2002), 1–18. Both are concerned with a diachronic reading of *ekphrasis* between classical and later periods; see also Simon Goldhill, "The Naïve and Knowing Eye: Ecphrasis and the Culture of Viewing in the Hellenistic World," in *Art and Text in Ancient Greek Culture*, ed. S. Goldhill and R. Osborne (Cambridge, UK: Cambridge University Press, 1994), 197–223. *Classical Philology* 102, no. 1 (2007) is a special issue devoted to *ekphrasis* edited by Shadi Bartsch and Jaś Elsner (not confined to art history). For *ekphrasis* in Byzantium see Dagron, *Décrire et peindre*, 83–109.

36. As described by Ruth Webb, "Accomplishing the Picture: Ekphrasis, Mimesis and Martyrdom in Asterios of Amaseia," in *Art and Text in Byzantine Culture*, ed. James, 13–33, at 14; for *ekphrasis* as rivaling visual art rather than describing it, see ibid., 16. A notable Byzantine example is the tenth-century account of the monuments of Constantinople and the church of the Holy Apostles by Constantine the Rhodian: Liz James, with Ioannis Vassis, ed., *Constantine of Rhodes, Constantinople and the Church of the Holy Apostles* (Farnham, UK: Ashgate, 2012).

37. This is brought out by Jaś Elsner, *Art and the Roman Viewer: The Transformation of Art from the Pagan World to Christianity* (Cambridge, UK: Cambridge University Press, 1995); cf. also id., *Roman Eyes: Visuality and Subjectivity in Art and Text* (Princeton, NJ: Princeton University Press, 2007); id., ed., *Art and Text in Roman Culture* (Cambridge, UK: Cambridge University Press, 1996).

38. This is less often connected with the use of patristic citations in theological writing; these are usually (and rightly) seen in terms of the appeal to authorities, but it would be interesting to explore their stylistic value as well.

39. For Riegl see W. Liebeschuez, "The Birth of Late Antiquity," *Ant. tard.* 12 (2004), 253–61; see also Jaś Elsner, "From the Culture of *Spolia* to the Cult of Relics: The Arch of Constantine and the Genesis of Late Antique Form," *PBSR* 68 (2000), 149–84; and from a literary point of view M. Formisano, "Towards an Aesthetic Paradigm of Late Antiquity," *Ant. tard.* 15 (2007), 277–84.

40. The Russian scholar Alexei Lidov identifies this conception of sacred space as "hierotopy"; and see Pentcheva, *The Sensual Icon*, with ead., "What Is a Byzantine Icon? Constantinople versus Sinai," in *The Byzantine World*, ed. Stephenson, 265–83; Robert S. Nelson, "Image and Inscription: Pleas for Salvation in Spaces of Devotion," in *Art and Text*, ed. James, 100–119.

41. Nelson, "Image and Inscription," 109, who also says that icons "transform the spaces of their performance."

42. For a model of such exegesis, applied to *vita*-icons of the early thirteenth century associated with Sinai and representing a possible "mode of transmission" between cultures in the Eastern Mediterranean, using "the one truly international language . . . namely the language of art," see Nancy Patterson Ševčenko, "The 'Vita-icon' and the Painter as Hagiographer," *DOP* 53 (1999), 149–65.

43. See the essays in Dan Hicks and Mary C. Beaudrey, eds., *The Oxford Handbook of Material Culture Studies* (Oxford, UK: Oxford University Press, 2010); Hicks discusses the "material-culture turn," in chapter 2, 26–98. An online bibliography on Byzantine material culture can be found at www.univie.ac.at/byzantine (Michael Grünbart), accessed 05.09.2013; and see M. Grünbart,"Bibliography on Byzantine Material Culture and Daily Life," *Byzantinoslavica* 67 (2009), 13–16; with M. Grünbart and D. Stathakopoulos, "Sticks and Stones: Byzantine Material Culture," *BMGS* 26 (2002), 298–327 (with some methodological remarks at 304 f.).

44. See A. M. Jones and N. Boivin, in Hicks and Beaudrey, earlier, 340–42.

Chapter 5. The Very Model of Orthodoxy?

1. See F. Fukuyama, *The End of History and the Last Man* (New York: Free Press, 1992); Fukuyama explains and defends himself in "Reflections on *The End of History*, Five Years Later," *History and Theory* 34, no. 2 (1995), 27–43.

"Orthodox civilization" is defined negatively by Samuel Huntington and others, by its supposed lack of the features allegedly constitutive of western Europe, including a Renaissance and an Enlightenment; there is an inescapable resonance here with western attitudes toward the east, and toward Islam in particular (chapter 2).

2. This translates into politics, obviously in Russia, but also in relation to Greece and its relation with Serbia.

3. A general introduction is provided in the thoughtful contribution of Mary Cunningham, "Byzantine Views of God and the Universe," in *A Companion to Byzantium*, ed. Liz James (Chichester, UK: Wiley-Blackwell, 2010), 149–60, especially her conclusions, with a conspectus of the basic bibliography.

4. Well described by Warren T. Woodfin, "Celestial Hierarchies and Earthly Hierarchies in the Art of the Byzantine Church," in *The Byzantine World*, ed. Paul Stephenson (London: Routledge, 2010), 303–19. The fifth- or sixth-century writings of Ps. Dionysius the Areopagite on celestial and ecclesiastical hierarchies provided an underpinning, but the idea went back even earlier.

5. The patriarch of Constantinople was not the only one: the doctrine of a "pentarchy" (that is, the patriarchates of Rome, Constantinople, Antioch, Alexandria, and Jerusalem) expressed a continuity of understanding, despite political realities. A "standing synod" had also existed in the capital from an early date and could be summoned when required. But the patriarch of Constantinople occupied a special place in view of his relation to the emperor and the capital.

6. A fuller statement of this position, based on the early period, can be found in Averil Cameron, "The Cost of Orthodoxy," *Church History and Religious Culture* 93.3 (2013), 339–61.

7. Paul Magdalino, "Orthodoxy and Byzantine Cultural Identity," in *Orthodoxy and Heresy in Byzantium: The Definition and the Notion of Orthodoxy and Some Other Studies on the Heresies and the Non-Christian Religions*, ed. A. Rigo and P. Ermilov, Quaderni di *Nea Rhome* 4 (Rome, 2010), 21–46, responding to my "Byzantium and the Limits of Orthodoxy," Raleigh Lecture in History, *Proceedings of the British Academy* 154 (2008), 139–52.

8. For this lengthy document, drawn up to be read out annually during the

liturgy, see J. Gouillard, "Le Synodikon d'Orthodoxie. Édition et commentaire," *TM* 2 (1967), 1–316. Charles Barber, *Contesting the Logic of Painting: Art and Understanding in Eleventh-century Byzantium* (Leiden: Brill, 2007), chapter 1, brilliantly draws on the surviving *Synaxarion* of the monastery of the Theotokos Evergetis in Constantinople (which prescribes the monastery's liturgical readings) in order to re-create the effects of the annual reading of the *Synodikon.*

9. See Patricia Karlin-Hayter, "Methodios and His Synod," in *Byzantine Orthodoxies*, ed. Andrew Louth and Augustine Casiday (Aldershot, UK: Ashgate, 2006), 55–74, demonstrates the many ambiguities surrounding the supposed watershed of AD 843.

10. For doubts about this idea, and for references, see Matthew Dal Santo and Phil Booth, "Conclusion," in *An Age of Saints? Power, Conflict and Dissent in Early Medieval Christianity*, ed. Peter Sarris, Matthew Dal Santo, and Phil Booth (Leiden: Brill, 2011), 205–14, at 205–7.

11. See Katerina Ierodiakonou, ed., *Byzantine Philosophy and Its Ancient Sources* (Oxford, UK: Clarendon Press, 2002); and Börje Bydén and Katerina Ierodiakonou, eds., *The Many Faces of Byzantine Philosophy* (Athens: Norwegian Institute at Athens, 2012), especially the introductory essays by Ierodiakonou in each volume. As Ierodiakonou points out (2012), the reception of the first book makes clear the persistence of existing assumptions, and the controversial nature of such challenges. While it may be argued that it would be premature as yet, a new history of Byzantine philosophy is much needed.

12. See Sarris, Dal Santo, and Booth, eds., *An Age of Saints?*; and see A. Kaldellis, "Byzantine Philosophy Inside and Out: Orthodoxy and Dissidence in Counterpoint," in *The Many Faces of Byzantine Philosophy*, ed. Bydén and Ierodiakonou, 129–53.

13. Paul Magdalino uses the memorable term "The Guardians of Orthodoxy" as the chapter heading for his wide-ranging discussion in *The Empire of Manuel I Komnenos, 1143–1180* (Cambridge, UK: Cambridge University Press, 1993), 316–412. Orthodoxy certainly needed guardians even if they did not necessarily agree about what they were guarding; I am less convinced by Magdalino's choice of heading (within a chapter on "Government": "Church and State," 267–309).

14. This is still true in the case of Louth and Casiday, eds., *Byzantine Orthodoxies*, which ends with a paper by S. Averintsev with the title "Some Constant Characteristics of Byzantine Orthodoxy." Contrast for example the review of two recent collective volumes on early Christianity by J. Rüpke, "Early Christianity out of, and in, Context," *JRS* 99 (2009), 182–83; and the papers in A.-C. Jacobsen, J. Ulrich, and D. Brakke, eds., *Invention, Rewriting, Usurpations: Discursive Fights over Religious Traditions in Antiquity* (Frankfurt am Main: Peter Lang, 2011).

15. The central study of these tensions is G. Dagron, *Emperor and Priest: The Imperial Office in Byzantium*, Eng. trans. (Cambridge, UK: Cambridge University Press, 2003).

16. S. Papaioannou, *Michael Psellos. Rhetoric and Authorship in Byzantium* (Cambridge, UK: Cambridge University Press, 2013), 52.

17. G. Dagron, "La règle et l'exception. Analyse de la notion de l'économie," in *Religiöse Devianz. Untersuchungen zu sozialen, rechtlichen und theologischen Reaktionen auf religiöse Abweichung im westlichen und östlichen Mittelalter*, ed. D. Simon (Frankfurt am Main: Klostermann, 1990), 1–19.

18. See Papaioannou, *Michael Psellos*, chapter 1.

19. The deep ambivalence felt in Byzantium toward applying Aristotelian logic to theological argument despite the fact that Aristotle's logic was taught throughout the period is brought out by Katerina Ierodiakonou, "The Anti-logical Movement in the Fourteenth Century," in ead., ed., *Byzantine Philosophy and Its Ancient Sources*, 219–35.

20. *Alexiad*, V.2, trans. E.R.A. Sewter, rev. Peter Frankopan (London: Penguin Classics, 2009), 130–32.

21. Eustratius, *Dialogue on the Veneration of Icons*, ed. A. Demetrakopoulos, *Ekklesiastike Bibliotheke*, I (Leipzig, 1866), 127–51; according to Nicetas Choniates, Eustratius often took part in imperial debates with Latins on azymes (the use by the Latins of unleavened bread in the Eucharist) and the *filioque*, and debated with the Armenians when he accompanied Alexius when the latter was on campaign at Philippopolis (*Thes.*, XXIII, PG 140.136–37). Anna Comnena, the patron of his Aristotelian commentaries, described him as "more confident in dialectic than those who frequent the Stoa and the Academy" (*Alexiad*, XIV.8).

22. Greek text and Latin translation, *PG* 127.972–984D. The episode is discussed from the viewpoint of art history by Charles Barber, *Contesting the Logic of Painting: Art and Understanding in Eleventh-Century Byzantium* (Leiden: Brill, 2007), chapters 4 and 5.

23. They included 48 members of the senate, 24 metropolitans and archbishops, 8 ecclesiastical "archontes," and 15 heads of monasteries: see P. Gautier, "Le synode de Blachernes (fin 1094). Étude prosopographique," *REB* 29 (1971), 213–84.

24. Anathemas proclaimed on those considered heretical went back at least as far as the early fourth century: see Rosemary Morris, "Curses and Clauses: The Language of Repression in Byzantium," in *Toleration and Repression in the Middle Ages: In Memory of Lenos Mavromattis*. ed. K. Nikolaou (Athens, 2002), 313–26.

25. Cited by Jaś Elsner, "Iconoclasm as Discourse: From Antiquity to Byzantium," *Art Bulletin* 94, no. 3 (2012), 368–94, at 380.

26. Ed Demetrakopoulos, *Ekkl. Bibl.* I, 151–60. I am indebted to Foteini Spingou for her invaluable work in the context of my current project on Byzantine prose dialogues.

27. See P. Ioannou, "Eustrate de Nicée. Trois pieces inédits de son procès," *REB* 10 (1952), 24–34; the three items in question consist of the judgment of the patriarch, John IX Agapetos; the record of how each member of the synod voted; and the syllabus of errors, a list of twenty-four propositions constituting the grounds of which Eustratius was condemned.

28. The part of the *Synodikon* that concerns Eustratius is at lines 388 to 423, discussed by Gouillard at pp. 206–10.

29. Alexius's reign saw the condemnation of Eustratius's teacher, the Italian philosopher John Italus, and other show trials; the public burning of Basil, a Bogomil leader; legislation introducing major ecclesiastical reforms; and the commissioning of a major heresiological compendium, the *Dogmatic Panoply* by Euthymius Zigabenus.

30. See C. Simelidis, "The Byzantine Understanding of the Qur'anic Term *al-Samad* and the Greek Translation of the Qur'an," *Speculum* 86 (2011), 887–913, at 905–6.

31. Thomas Graumann, "The Conduct of Theology and the 'Fathers' of the

Church," in *A Companion to Late Antiquity*, ed. Philip Rousseau (Chichester, UK: Wiley-Blackwell, 2009), 539–55.

32. The last chapter is his famous discussion of Islam, which is presented as a Christian heresy. For a discussion of the *Fount of Knowledge* in its monastic context see Andrew Louth, *St. John Damascene: Tradition and Originality in Byzantine Theology* (Oxford, UK: Oxford University Press, 2001), chapters 3–6, in a section headed "Faith and Logic."

33. Magdalino, *The Empire of Manuel I Komnenos*, 367.

34. Ibid., 367–68.

35. For the process see the comprehensive work of H. Inglebert, *Interpretatio Christiana. Les mutations des savoirs (cosmographie, géographie, ethnographie, histoire) dans l'Antiquité chrétienne, 30–630 après J.C.* (Paris: Institut d'études augustiniennes, 2001). Heresiology developed early into a literary genre in its own right, as argued in my "How to Read Heresiology," in *The Cultural Turn in Late Ancient Studies: Gender, Asceticism, and Historiography*, ed. Dale Martin and Patricia Cox Miller (Durham, NC: Duke University Press, 2005), 193–212.

36. Magdalino, *Empire of Manuel I Komnenos*, 366 f.

37. Though legal expertise was prized and highly developed, and can be seen in action at certain periods: see for instance Leonora Neville, *Authority in Byzantine Provincial Society, 950–1100* (Cambridge, UK: Cambridge University Press, 2004).

38. According to Peter Brown, "A Dark-Age Crisis: Aspects of the Iconoclast Controversy," *EHR* 88, no. 346 (1973), 1–34, Byzantine iconoclasm was a reaction to the centrifugal force represented by monks and holy men.

39. This is compounded by the level of *parti pris* in existing scholarship (chapter 1), noted also in relation to the controversy between Barlaam and Palamas in the fourteenth century by Ierodiakonou, "The Anti-logical Movement," 233.

40. See P. Magdalino, "Orthodoxy and Byzantine Cultural Identity"; id., "Orthodoxy and Heresy in Tenth-Century Byzantine 'Encyclopaedism,'" in *Encyclopaedic Trends in Byzantium*, ed. P. Van Deun and C. Macé, Orientalia Lovaniensia Analecta 212 (Leuven: Peeters, 2011), 143–59, arguing for an orthodox agenda behind Constantine VII Porphyrogenitus's compilations (cf.

p. 151, "an orthodox culture is by nature normative and prescriptive"; p. 154, "the encyclopaedism of the tenth century was an imperial appropriation . . . of a religious ideology of law and order that had been developed by the monastic reformation of the eighth and ninth centuries in connection with the Triumph of Orthodoxy").

41. Magdalino, "Orthodoxy and Byzantine Cultural Identity," 25–26.

42. See Averil Cameron and Robert Hoyland, eds., *Doctrine and Debate in the East Christian World, 300–1500* (Farnham, UK: Ashgate, 2011), introduction; and cf. the papers in S. Elm, É. Rebillard, and A. Romano, eds., *Orthodoxie, christianisme, histoire* (Rome: École française de Rome, 2000); contrast Magdalino, "Orthodoxy and Byzantine Cultural Identity," 34, referring to "the seventh and eighth centuries, when Orthodox doctrine was being defined."

43. The term "culture" also features in the title of Denis Sullivan, Elizabeth Fisher, and Stratis Papaioannou, eds., *Byzantine Religious Culture: Studies in Honor of Alice-Mary Talbot* (Leiden: Brill, 2012).

44. Magdalino, "Orthodoxy and Byzantine Cultural Identity," 32; cf. M. Whittow, *The Making of Orthodox Byzantium, 650–1025* (London: Macmillan, 1996), 139–64.

45. Magdalino, "Orthodoxy and Byzantine Cultural Identity," 35. Magdalino connects the intellectual endeavors and patronage of Leo VI and Constantine VII with this urge to restore orthodoxy (and refers to Byzantium as a "theocracy" in id., "Knowledge in Authority and Authorized History: The Imperial Intellectual Programme of Leo VI and Constantine VII," in *Authority in Byzantium*, ed. Pamela Armstrong (Farnham, UK: Ashgate, 2013), 187–209, at 194.

46. See for example Alexander P. Kazhdan and Giles Constable, *People and Power in Byzantium: An Introduction to Modern Byzantine Studies* (Washington, DC: Dumbarton Oaks, 1982).

47. These included for instance the *Horos* (statement) agreed by the iconophile council of 787, read out in October each year.

48. See Jill Harries, "Superfluous Verbiage? Rhetoric and Law in the Age of Constantine and Julian," *Journal of Early Christian Studies* 19, no. 3 (2011), 345–74, and other works cited there.

Epilogue

1. Johann P. Arnason, "Byzantium and Historical Sociology," in *The Byzantine World*, ed. Paul Stephenson (London: Routledge, 2010), 491–504, at 497 (from a thoughtful essay, many of whose arguments I would endorse).

2. Ibid., 496.

3. Ibid., 497–98.

FURTHER READING

Introduction

James, Liz, ed., *A Companion to Byzantium* (Chichester, UK: Wiley-Blackwell, 2010).

Jeffreys, Elizabeth, John F. Haldon, Robin Cormack, eds., *The Oxford Handbook of Byzantine Studies* (New York: Oxford University Press, 2008).

Mango, Cyril, ed., *The Oxford History of Byzantium* (Oxford, UK: Oxford University Press, 2002).

Shepard, Jonathan, ed., *The Cambridge History of the Byzantine Empire* (Cambridge, UK: Cambridge University Press, 2008).

Stephenson, Paul, ed., *The Byzantine World* (London: Routledge, 2010).

Chapter 1. Absence

Browning, Robert, *Medieval and Modern Greek*, 2nd ed. (Cambridge, UK: Cambridge University Press, 1983).

Cameron, Averil, *The Byzantines* (Oxford, UK: Blackwell, 2006).

———, *The Mediterranean World in Late Antiquity, 395–700 AD*, rev. and expanded ed. (London: Routledge, 2012).

———, "Old and New Rome: Roman Studies in Sixth-Century Constantinople," in *Transformations of Late Antiquity: Essays for Peter Brown*, ed. Philip Rousseau and Manolis Papoutsakis (Farnham, UK: Ashgate, 2009), 15–36.

Haldon, John F., *The Palgrave Atlas of Byzantine History* (Basingstoke, UK: Macmillan, 2005.

Kazhdan, Alexander P., Alice-Mary Talbot, Anthony Cutler, Timothy E.

Gregory, and Nancy P. Ševčenko, eds., *The Oxford Dictionary of Byzantium*, 3 vols. (New York: Oxford University Press, 1991).
Stephenson, Paul, "Byzantium's European Future," in *The Byzantine World*, ed. P. Stephenson (London: Routledge, 2010), 505–9.

The many volumes in the series known as the *Tabula Imperii Byzantini* (*TIB*), published by the Vienna Academy, provide detailed historical maps and are an indispensable guide to topography and settlement in the territories of the Byzantine empire.

Special mention should also be made of the important role played in opening up the field of Byzantine studies by the many projects and publications of the Byzantine Research Center at Dumbarton Oaks, Washington, DC (Harvard University).

Chapter 2. Empire

Ahrweiler, Hélène, and Angeliki E. Laiou, eds., *Studies on the Internal Diaspora of the Byzantine Empire* (Washington, DC: Dumbarton Oaks, 1998).
Angelov, Dimiter, *Imperial Ideology and Political Thought in Byzantium, 1204–1330* (Cambridge, UK: Cambridge University Press, 2007).
Cameron, Averil, "Gibbon and Justinian," in *Edward Gibbon and Empire*, ed. Rosamond McKitterick and Roland Quinault (Cambridge, UK: Cambridge University Press, 1997), 34–52.
Haldon, John F., *Byzantium: A History* (Stroud, UK: Tempus, 2000), especially chapters 4 and 6.
Laiou, Angeliki E., *Byzantium and the Other: Relations and Exchanges*, ed. Cécile Morrisson and Rowan Dorin (Farnham, UK: Ashgate, 2012).
Laiou, Angeliki E., and Henry Maguire, eds., *Byzantium: A World Civilization* (Washington, DC: Dumbarton Oaks, 1992).
Magdalino, Paul, *Constantinople médiévale: études sur l'évolution des structures urbaines* (Paris: De Boccard, 1996).
Magdalino, Paul, ed., *New Constantines: The Rhythm of Imperial Renewal in Byzantium, 4th to 13th Centuries* (Aldershot, UK: Variorum, 1994).

Mango, Cyril, *Le développement urbain de Constantinople (IVe–VIIe siècles)*, rev. ed. (Paris: Boccard, 1990).

Mango, Cyril, Gilbert Dagron, and Geoffrey Greatrex, eds., *Constantinople and Its Hinterland* (Aldershot, UK: Variorum, 1995).

Morrisson, Cécile, Jean-Claude Cheynet, and Angeliki E. Laiou, eds., *Le monde byzantin*, 3 vols. (Paris: Presses Universitaires de France, 2004–).

Sarris, Peter, *Empires of Faith: The Fall of Rome to the Rise of Islam, 500–700*, The Oxford History of Medieval Europe (Oxford, UK: Oxford University Press, 2011).

Treadgold, Warren T., *A History of the Byzantine State and Society* (Stanford, CA: Stanford University Press, 1997).

Chapter 3. Hellenism

Argyropoulos, Roxane D., *Les intellectuels grecs à la recherche de Byzance (1860–1912)* (Athens: Institut de recherches néohelléniques, 2001).

Clogg, Richard, *Politics and the Academy: Arnold Toynbee and the Koraes Chair* (London: Frank Cass, 1986).

Guran, Petre, "Late Antiquity in Byzantium," in *The Oxford Handbook of Late Antiquity*, ed. Scott Fitzgerald Johnson (New York: Oxford University Press, 2012), 1148–71.

Millar, Fergus, *A Greek Roman Empire: Power and Belief under Theodosius II (408–50)* (Berkeley: University of California Press, 2006).

Mullett, Margaret, and Roger Scott, eds., *Byzantium and the Classical Tradition* (Birmingham, UK: Centre for Byzantine Studies, University of Birmingham, 1981).

Ricks, David, and Paul Magdalino, eds., *Byzantium and the Modern Greek Identity* (Aldershot, UK: Ashgate, 1998).

Saïd, Suzanne, ed., *Hellenismos. Quelques jalons pour une histoire de l'identité grecque*. Actes du Colloque de Strasbourg, 25–27 Oct. 1989 (Leiden: Brill, 1990).

Zacharia, Katerina, ed., *Hellenisms: Culture, Identity and Ethnicity from Antiquity to Modernity* (Aldershot, UK: Ashgate, 2008).

Chapter 4. The Realms of Gold

Belting, Hans, *Bild und Kunst. Eine Geschichte der Bilder vor dem Zeitalter der Kunst* (Munich: Beck, 1990); Eng. trans., E. Jephcott, *Likeness and Presence: A History of the Image before the Era of Art* (Chicago: University of Chicago Press, 1994).

Cameron, Averil, *The Use and Abuse of Byzantium*, Inaugural Lecture, King's College London, 1990 (London, 1992); reprinted in *Changing Cultures in Early Byzantium* (Aldershot, UK: Variorum, 1996), no. XIII.

Cormack, Robin, *Painting the Soul: Icons, Death Masks and Shrouds* (London: Reaktion Books, 1997).

———, *Writing in Gold: Byzantine Society and Its Icons* (London: George Philip, 1985).

Elsner, Jaś, "Iconoclasm as Discourse: From Antiquity to Byzantium," *The Art Bulletin* 94, no. 3 (September 2012), 368–94.

Mango, Cyril, ed., *The Art of the Byzantine Empire, 312–1453: Sources and Documents* (Englewood Cliffs, NJ: Prentice Hall, 1972).

Chapter 5. The Very Model of Orthodoxy?

Angold, Michael, ed., *Eastern Christianity*, Cambridge History of Christianity 5 (Cambridge, UK: Cambridge University Press, 2006).

Beck, Hans-Georg, *Kirche und theologische Literatur im byzantinischen Reich* (Munich: Beck, 1959).

Cameron, Averil, and Robert G. Hoyland, eds., *Doctrine and Debate in the East Christian World, 300–1500* (Farnham, UK: Ashgate, 2011).

Dagron, Gilbert, Pierre Riché, and André Vauchez, eds., with the collaboration of Christian Hannick, *Evêques, moines et empereurs, 610–1054, Histoire du christianisme des origines à nos jours* (Paris: Desclée, 1993).

Hatlie, Peter, *The Monks and Monasteries of Constantinople, ca. 350–850* (Cambridge, UK: Cambridge University Press, 2007).

Krueger, Derek, *Byzantine Christianity*, People's History of Christianity 3 (Minneapolis, MN: Fortress Press, 2006).

Louth, Andrew, "The Emergence of Byzantine Orthodoxy, 600–1095," in *Early Medieval Christianities, ca. 600–ca. 1100*, The Cambridge History of Christianity 3, ed. Thomas F. X. Noble and Julia M. H. Smith (Cambridge, UK: Cambridge University Press, 2008), 46–94.

———, *Greek East and Latin West: The Church, AD 681–1071* (Crestwood, NY: St. Vladimir's Seminary Press, 2007).

Morris, Rosemary, *Monks and Laymen in Byzantium, 843–1118* (Cambridge, UK: Cambridge University Press, 1995).

Mullett, Margaret, ed., *Founders and Refounders of Byzantine Monasteries* (Belfast: Belfast Byzantine Enterprises, 2007).

AUTHOR'S NOTE

The following published and unpublished papers are relevant in different ways to some of the material in this book:

"The Absence of Byzantium," *Nea Hestia* Jan. 2008, 4–59 (English and Greek).

"Byzantium and the Limits of Orthodoxy," Raleigh Lecture in History, *Proceedings of the British Academy* 154 (2008), 139–52.

"Empire, Empires and the End of Antiquity," Ronald Syme Lecture, Wolfson College, Oxford, UK, 2010, unpublished.

"How Orthodox Was Byzantium?," Lecture, Oxford Centre for Byzantine Research, Oxford, UK, 2010, unpublished.

John W. Pope Lecture, University of North Carolina, Chapel Hill, NC, 2011, unpublished.

"Thinking with Byzantium," *Transactions of the Royal Historical Society* 21 (2011), 39–57.

"Byzantium Today," Lecture given in connection with the 125th anniversary of the British School at Athens, The British Academy, 2012, unpublished.

"Seeing Byzantium: A Personal Response," in *Wonderful Things: Byzantium through Its Art*, ed. Liz James and Antony Eastmond, Papers from the Forty-first Spring Symposium of Byzantine Studies, Courtauld Institute of Art and King's College, London, March 2009 (Farnham, UK: Ashgate, 2013), 311–18.

INDEX

Note: Page numbers in italic type indicate illustrations.